T0353657

Voices of Preachers in Protest

First Published by Kachere Series in 2001.

Published by
Luviri Press
P/Bag 201 Luwinga
Mzuzu 2

ISBN   978-99960-66-12-2
eISBN   978-99960-66-13-9

Luviri Reprints no. 11

Luviri Press is represented outside Malawi by:
African Books Collective Oxford (orders@africanbookscollective.com)

www.mzunipress.blogspot.com
www.africanbookscollective.com

Voices of Preachers in Protest

The Ministry of Two Malawian Prophets:
Elliot Kamwana and Wilfred Gudu

J.C. Chakanza

Luviri Press

Luviri Reprints no. 11
Mzuzu
2018

Luviri Reprints

Many books have been published on or in Malawi that are no longer available. While some of these books simply have run their course, others are still of interest for scholars and the general public. Some of the classics have been reprinted outside Malawi over the decades, and during the last two decades, first the Kachere Series and then other publishers have achieved "never out of stock status" by joining the African Books Collective's Print on Demand approach, but there are still a good number of books that would be of interest but are no longer in print.

The Luviri Reprint Series has taken up the task to make those books on or from Malawi, which are out of print but not out of interest, available again, through Print on Demand and therefore worldwide.

While the Luviri Reprint Series concentrates on Malawi, it is also interested in the neighbouring countries and even in those further afield.

Luviri Reprints publish the books as they originally were. Usually a new Foreword is added, and where appropriate, new information has been added. All such additions, mostly in footnotes, are marked by an asterisk (*).

The Editors

Contents

Series Editors' Preface

The Kachere Series is an initiative of the Department of Theology and Religious Studies at the University of Malawi. It aims to promote the emergence of a body of literature which will enable students and others to engage critically with religion in Malawi, its social impact and the theological questions which it raises. An important starting point lies with the publication of essays and theses which until now have been inaccessible to all but the most dedicated specialist. It is also hoped, however, that the development of theological scholarship in Malawi will stimulate the writing of many new books. General works with popular appeal can be published as *Kachere Books*. Documents and essays, which are of value as sources for the study of religion in Malawi, can be published as *Kachere Texts*. It is in the third branch of the series, known as *Kachere Monographs*, that full-length academic treatises are published. Only the fruits of sound primary research which meet rigorous academic standards will be accepted for publication in this prestigious branch of the Series. The Editors intend the Monographs to contribute substantially to the growth of a body of knowledge in the area of theology and religious studies in Malawi. As important resources for study related to this field, we are confident that they will come to be prized not only within Malawi but in every academic centre concerned with religion and society in Africa.

This monograph addresses the issue of religious protest in Malawi by two founders of African Instituted Churches during the colonial period. Elliot Kenan Kamwana from Nkhata Bay in the North started as an emissary of the Watch Tower Movement from South Africa in 1908 and later founded the Watchman Healing Mission in 1937. His criticism focussed upon the Livingstonia Mission and the colonial government. Wilfrid Gudu from Thyolo in the South, founded the Ana a Mulungu church in 1935. His grievances were also aimed against the colonial administrators and against the traditional rulers. The author has concentrated on their significant events, developments and experiences and attempts to place the movements and their founders in a larger framework by assessing their beliefs and impact so as to enlarge the appeal of the work. This study has made extensive use of primary sources not previously used by historians of Malawi and some not available in archives overseas. There is still much oral data untapped on these, and many other churches. It is hoped that this study will contribute to the growing knowledge and understanding of the role played by the African Instituted Churches in the social, political and religious transformation of Malawi.

We thank The Pew Charitable Trust for their assistance in financing this research, Dean Hans Blum for allowing us to reproduce the cover illustration and Celeste M. Geddes for producing the index and transforming the manuscript into camera ready copy.

Kachere Series Editors
Zomba, April 1998

List of Maps and Photographs

Maps

Photographs

Introduction

The colonial context in Malawi within which nearly one hundred African Instituted Churches (AICs) originated, and David Barrett's thesis concerning the "failure in love" on the part of the mission churches, focus upon the AICs in terms of "reaction" This approach, fails to emphasize the positive and dynamic religious thrust which is intrinsic to these movements. In this case study of the ministry of two select Malawian "prophets", Elliot Kenan Kamwana and Wilfrid Gudu, I have tried to pay attention to their religious experiences as founders and leaders of new religious movements in their time and place to account for their phenomenal success in attracting large numbers of followers.

The AICs in general must be seen as valid and genuine expressions of religious initiative and creativity with a missionary thrust in their own right. They are also a positive response to a widespread religious need among African peoples, a response which is given within the framework of the Bible, and which is fulfilling a need not being satisfied elsewhere. "Liberation" or "salvation" is seen as including a striving for freedom from alien religious leadership and culturally alien forms of religious belief and practice. The general conviction is that God has ever been present among His people, just as He has been in all peoples, cultures and religious tendencies of the world, not just as condescension, but because His benevolent presence is in the logic of the cosmic covenant of creation and re-creation. Therefore the question of salvation is seen from a holistic standpoint in which full account is taken, not only of the special choices of elections of God, but also of all other elements in God's relations with the whole of mankind.

Kamwana and Gudu as preachers, "prophets", and founders of new movements, articulated eloquently their followers' response to the tightening grip of colonialism with its oppressive policies on certain pertinent issues in the wake of the introduction of a capitalist economy. The integrity of the Christian missions in upholding the people's rights against violation by the colonial government and in the practical implementation of equity and justice within their domain, was questioned and even challenged

9

because of some inconsistencies. In a number of cases the missionaries showed little understanding of the people's plight and were insensitive to their aspirations, partly because of their uncompromising stance against some aspects of traditional culture.

Kamwana, whose ministry was in two phases (1908-1909; 1937-1956) shows a remarkable change in his religious convictions and orientation from one to the other. During the first phase he operated under the broadly-based Watch Tower Movement and in the second phase he founded the Watchman Healing Mission. He was based in his home district, Nkhata Bay in the Northern Region, within the Livingstonia Mission's sphere of influence, and from where he supervised the various branches of his movement throughout the country. Gudu's ministry, on the other hand, was confined mainly to his home district, Thyolo, in the Southern Region, then in the throes of an expanding plantation economy and immigration of the Lomwe from neighbouring Mozambique. The most influential Mission in the area was the Seventh-day Adventist Malamulo Mission (Plainfield), of which he had initially become a member. The acute pressure on land, the agricultural reform policies, the low wages paid to workers on the estates, and the partiality showed by the Seventh-day Adventist missionaries in matters affecting their church members, all contributed to Gudu's grievances. While Kamwana's ministry was concerned with issues of national and pan-African aspirations due partly to his exposure to the outside world, his home area, Nkhata Bay, did not experience the problems of land alienation, immigration and a cash economy as did Thyolo. Therefore his main grievances at home were centred around some of Livingstonia Mission's policies.

Both Kamwana and Gudu came into conflict with the colonial authorities and with the missionaries who had brought them up. This led to imprisonment and temporary banishment from their home districts: Kamwana, the more outspoken of the two, to the Seychelles while Gudu languished in Zomba Prison. This persecution not only strengthened them in their determination to flaunt the authority of the government and the missions, but also turned them into "charismatic" figures in the eyes of their followers. Although their main grievances were principally the same - the oppressive character of the colonial system shown in a number of ways and some policies and activities of the missions which appeared to have contradicted

10

what they stood for - their approach to these issues and the solutions they offered or adopted, differed in certain aspects. To start with, Kamwana, during his ministry, had adopted the Russellite Watch Tower millennarian doctrine and transformed it to apply to the prevailing conditions in the country and in colonial Africa as a whole. After his return from exile, his political militancy and pan-Africanism seem to have toned down and he became pre-occupied with the religious concerns of the Watchman Healing Mission, the new movement he had founded. Gudu, on the other hand, made his accusations against government officials and missionaries on specific issues and does not appear to have been under the influence of either militant nationalism or pan-Africanism. In the end however, both Kamwana and Gudu felt that forming separate religious communities where their members would share their faith experiences without disturbance from the "world", would signify symbolically the anticipated state of peace and calm. Understandably, it was in this context that the two preachers developed the characteristics of a prophet.

In compiling and writing up these case-studies, I have relied heavily on my own field notes, archival resources, seminar papers and some other primary sources given to me by students and other interested people. In my interpretation, evaluation and analysis of the events that took place, I have tried to situate them in the people's traditional milieux and ways of understanding, something which seems to be lacking in much of the published material on Christianity in Malawi.

I wish to thank Mr Gideon Stivini from Molere, Thyolo, the immediate successor of Gudu, who kindly offered to write down for me the life and visionary experiences of Gudu which I have referred to on many occasions. Prof. J.M. Schoffeleers from Leiden, Holland, deserves my thanks for supplying me with material on Gudu and Kamwana from his own research notes. Finally my thanks go to many other people who have helped me in one way or another to complete this task, and here I mention specifically Dr Chijere Chirwa's undergraduate seminar paper on Kamwana, which has helped me to better understand the context in which he carried out his ministry.

Joseph Chaphadzika Chakanza
Eastertime, 1998

Part I: From Preacher to Prophet: Elliot Kenan Kamwana and the Watch Tower Movement in Malawi, 1908-1956

Of all the founders of religious or quasi-religious movements in Malawi, and perhaps also in Central Africa since the introduction of the missions, Elliot Kenan Kamwana has undoubtedly been the most influential. The only person to compare with him is Kamwendo, founder of the famous witchcraft eradication movement called *Mchape*[1] which, although short-lived, had a comparable impact on Central African societies in the 1930s. We know practically nothing about the founder of *Mchape* and relatively little about Kamwana, but there is plenty of information about their movements.

The history of Kamwana is rather patchy and almost totally lacking in analysis. While some authors, notably Sholto Cross,[2] have attempted an analysis of the movement, nobody has tried to come to any understanding regarding the man himself. By far the most often cited source is Shepperson and Price,[3] who devote a section of a chapter to Kamwana's activities between 1900 and 1917, the year of his deportation to the Seychelles. R.J. MacDonald gives an account of Kamwana's early life and the impact he made in northern Malawi.[4] Pachai has recorded systematically the significant dates in Kamwana's career from 1909 to his final deportation in 1917.[5] For a deeper understanding of the rise of the Watch Tower Movement in northern Malawi, McCracken discusses the inconsistencies in the

---

[1] For comparison of the *Mchape* movement with Watch Tower, see Sholto Cross, "The Watch Tower, Witch-cleansing and Secret Societies in Central Africa", paper read at Lusaka Conference on the History of Central African Religions, 1974.

[2] Sholto Cross, "The Watch Tower Movement in South Central Africa 1908-45", unpublished D. Phil., Oxon., 1973.

[3] George Shepperson and Thomas Price, *Independent African: John Chilembwe and the Origins, Setting and Significance of the Nyasaland Native Rising of 1915*, Edinburgh: Edinburgh University Press, 1958.

[4] R.J. MacDonald, "A History of African Education in Nyasaland 1875-1945", unpublished Ph.D., Edinburgh, 1969.

[5] Bridglal Pachai, "The State and the Churches in Malawi During Early Protectorate Rule", *Journal of Social Science*, (Malawi), Vol. 1 (1972), pp. 7-27.

Livingstonia Mission's policies which paved the way for Kamwana's success.[6] After this text was first written, Harry Langworthy published his biography of Joseph Booth, in which he treats Kamwana in various contexts.[7]

Three seminar papers written by J.D. Manda, B.M.N. Phiri and W. Ndopa Chijere Chirwa[8] respectively, are the only sources of more detailed information on Kamwana's activities after he had returned from exile. They suggest a rich store of oral data in Nkhata Bay but are sadly lacking in accuracy, with the exception of W. Chirwa.

Hooker,[9] Ranger,[10] Sholto Cross,[11] Greschat[12] and others are good on the spread of the movement outside Malawi, particularly in the mining areas of Southern Africa such as the Copperbelt in Zambia, the colliery in Hwange, the Rand in South Africa and also in the Katanga Province of Zaire.[13] No one has written on the spread of the movement inside Malawi, particularly towards the South such as the Lower Shire Valley

In this case study I shall discuss the following issues: Kamwana's early life; his first ministry from September 1908 to March 1909; the state of the

---

[6] John K. McCracken, *Politics and Christianity in Malawi 1875-1940*, London: Cambridge University Press, 1977.

[7] Harry Langworthy, *"Africa for the African": The Life of Joseph Booth*, Blantyre: CLAIM, 1996, for details see index on p. 509. Langworthy claims not to bring any new interpretation of Kamwana, only to add a few details. He reports that Kamwana married Annie Nyamanda in late 1908 (p. 207).

[8] J.D. Manda, "Independency in Nkhata Bay area from about 1930 to Current Times", History seminar paper, Zomba: Chancellor College, 1990; B.M.N. Phiri, "Independent Churches in Nkhata Bay District", History seminar paper, Zomba: Chancellor College, 1970; Wiseman Ndopa Chijere Chirwa, "Masokwa Elliot Kenan Kamwana Chirwa: His Religious and Political Activities, and the Effects of Kamwanaism in South-east Nkhata Bay, 1908-1956", History seminar paper, Zomba: Chancellor College, 1984.

[9] J.R. Hooker, "Witnesses and Watch Tower in the Rhodesias and Nyasaland", *Journal of African History*, Vol. VI/I (1965), pp. 91-106.

[10] T.O. Ranger, *The African Churches of Tanzania*, Historical Association of Tanzania, paper no. 5, Nairobi: East African Publishing House, n.d.

[11] Sholto Cross, "Social History and Millennial Movements: The Watch Tower in South Central Africa", *Social Compass*, Vol. XXIV (1977), pp. 83-95.

[12] Hans-Jürgen Greschat, "Kitawala, the Origins, Expansion and Religious Beliefs of the Watch Tower Movement in Central Africa", unpublished, Ph.D., Marburg, 1967. The English translation of this thesis is available at the Centre for the Study of New Religious Movements, Selly Oak Colleges, Birmingham, United Kingdom and in the Kachere Research Institute of the Department of Theology and Religious Studies, University of Malawi.

[13] Now the Democratic Republic of Congo.

Watch Tower Movement during his exile between 1909 and 1937; and his second ministry after exile from 1937 to 1956. In assessing his impact in Central Africa while focussing on Malawi, I shall raise the following questions:

(a) What was the essence of Kamwana's doctrine, and in what way was it different from the Russellite orthodoxy?

(b) Why and how did the change from Russellite orthodoxy come about?

(c) What other interpretation can be given of his movement, besides that which claims that it was an anti-colonialist protest?

(d) What changed Kamwana from preacher to prophet?

It is hoped that this analysis will lead to a deeper understanding of the phenomenal career of this preacher turned prophet.

(i) Early Life

The full name given to him by many sources is Elliot Kenan Kamwana Achirwa, but usually "Achirwa" is left out. However, Phiri gives Elliot Kenan Kamwana Masokwa Chirwa. He rightly states that the prefix "A" in the last name is honorific, and that the usual rendering is "Chirwa" The name "Masokwa", not mentioned by other writers, is explained by Phiri as given to children born before, or soon after, the death of an important member of the family, e.g. mother, father, grandparent, etc. Its literal meaning is "misfortune" [14]

It is generally accepted that Kamwana was born around 1882 at Mpopomeni Village in Mzimba District where his parents had been taken captives during the Ngoni raids.[15] His father was Mutemasalu Chirwa, and mother Agundankhuni Nyakuwera Nyamanda; but the name mentioned for his mother in the government file at Nkhata Bay is Nyathewera Nyaphiri. Phiri believes the name first mentioned is the correct one.

---

[14] Phiri, "Independent Churches in Nkhata Bay District", p. 1. See also Chirwa, "Masokwa Elliot Kenan Kamwana", p. 3.

[15] Oral communication: Mauritius Mangani Chirwa to Phiri, April 1968. Chirwa, ("Masokwa Elliot Kenan Kamwana Chirwa", p. 3) gives 1872. However MacDonald, ("A History of African Education in Nyasaland", p. 191) says that Kamwana was born between 1878 and 1882 at Chifira Village, Nkhata Bay District.

Mutemasalu became a war leader for the Ngoni. Being successful, he was murdered for fear that he would eventually take over the chieftaincy. Kamwana was born soon after this incident, and therefore was given the name "Masokwa"

Not long after the defeat of the Ngoni by the Tonga, his mother returned home to Chintheche at Chifira Village. When still young, probably in 1896, Kamwana went to live with his maternal uncle, Mtete, who worked as a works overseer (*kapitao*) for the African Lakes Corporation popularly known as "Mandala", at Karonga. Here, Mr Sildam (the white employer) called him "Kamwana", meaning "the little one", probably as a praise name for his cleverness.[16]

In the following year Kamwana returned to Chifira and started attending school at Sekela, Muyeyeka and Bandawe. It is there that he took the name "Elliot" In 1898, 'Stocken' (a missionary from Livingstonia) came to Bandawe to select pupils for the Overtoun Institution. Kamwana was among the few chosen. He became a pupil at the non-fee-paying Overtoun Institution from 1898 to 1901, attaining Standard III and finishing third in his class. However, he withdrew from the Institute, allegedly in protest at the introduction of school fees, as he had felt that education should be free.[17] The Rev. A. Macalpine maintained that Kamwana had actually been excommunicated because of unchastity.[18]

After leaving Overtoun, Kamwana set out for South Africa, but an outbreak of small-pox in Zimbabwe forced him to return and settle at Chinde, where he worked for Sharrer's Transport Company for seven months between 1901-1902. When he returned to Malawi he met Joseph Booth probably late in 1902, taught at Malamulo Mission and was baptized by Thomas Branch into the SDA Church.[19] From some time thereafter till June 1903, he taught under Joseph Booth and Thomas Branch at the Seventh-day Adventist Mission in Thyolo, which later came to be known as Malamulo Mission.

---

[16] Phiri, "Independent Churches in Nkhata Bay District", p. 2; Chirwa, "Masokwa Elliot Kamwana Chirwa", p. 4.

[17] *Livingstonia News*, Vol. 2/4 (October 1909), p. 59. 'Stocken' is almost certainly James Henderson, the Headmaster at the Overtoun Institution.

[18] *The Sabbath Recorder*, Vol. LXXIII/22 (1912), p. 719.

[19] Langworthy, *"Africa the African"*, p. 203.

During the second half of 1903, Kamwana left for South Africa, probably with Booth. For the next three years he was employed in Johannesburg, working for a while as time-keeper and hospital assistant in the mines. In the meanwhile, he was from time to time receiving papers from the headquarters of the Seventh-day Adventist Church in America and from the Watch Tower Bible and Tract Society of Alleghany, USA, which had a branch at Clifton-on-Sea near Cape Town. Joseph Booth, who had been to the USA in 1906 to see Russell, founder of the WTBTS, was the Society's agent in Cape Town. At his invitation, Kamwana went to Clifton-on-Sea from Johannesburg in early 1907 and was introduced to the Watch Tower doctrines until 7 July 1908. Thereafter, he preached for a few months, mainly in Johannesburg and also perhaps in Williamstown and Durban, before he was sent to Malawi in mid 1908 as an emissary of the Watch Tower Bible and Tract Society. After a brief attempt to preach at Shiloh outside Blantyre, still owned by Booth, Kamwana eventually returned to his home area, Chintheche, in Nkhata Bay District in November 1908.[20]

(ii)   First Ministry, 1908-1909

Kamwana's ministry in Malawi was in two phases. The first started in 1908 when he returned to Malawi as an emissary of the Watch Tower Bible and Tract Society. This lasted barely six months, after which he was removed from his home area and restricted to the southern Malawi districts until the colonial government eventually exiled him to the Seychelles in 1917. His movement suffered a temporary set-back but then began to spread to neighbouring districts and countries. The second phase started in 1937 when he was allowed to return home following the amnesty granted him on George VI's accession to the throne. He then dissociated himself from the Watch Tower Movement and started another religious organisation called the "Watchman Healing Mission"

I shall now turn my attention to Kamwana's six-month ministry between September 1908 and March 1909. According to contemporary Livingstonia Mission records, Kamwana started off his ministry by:

---

[20] Kamwana's account of himself as recorded by L.T. Moggridge, Resident, Chintheche, in a telegram to the Deputy Governor, 22 March 1909. See also Langworthy, *"Africa for the African"*, p. 205.

touring the whole Nkhata Bay District. He spoke cautiously with the people, noting carefully their desires and any dissatisfaction that existed among them and thus got a grip of the situation. He met privately elders of the church and the teachers and tried to persuade them to leave the missionaries and to take the work upon themselves.[21]

He apparently failed to lure away from the Free Church any significant numbers of its leading flock so that the *Livingstonia News* could report triumphantly:

> nowhere have well-instructed people been led away. Literature is posted from America every month to our leading teachers and it does no harm.[22]

Nevertheless, Kamwana found an intense desire for baptism and some discontent because the Church insisted on a lengthy course of instruction before baptism, and baptized only those who gave evidence of change of heart. The Livingstonia Mission admitted publicly that:

> a large number of catechumens have to be suspended and comparatively few are restored. Our system of having a long probation and attendance in instruction is proved to be the most wise one.[23]

Moreover, this policy was in line with the recommendation adopted by the first Nyasaland Missionary Conference of 1900 which stated that:

> baptism be not granted unless the candidate has been under definite religious instruction throughout a period of at least two years, during which the missionary has had means of ascertaining as to his life and character.[24]

Two years later, Elmslie took this policy a stage further among the Ngoni of Ekwendeni by refusing to baptize those who could not read the New

---

[21] R.D. McMinn, "The First Wave of Ethiopianism", *Livingstonia News*, Vol. 2/4 (October 1909), p. 57. Kamwana argued that once a person has been baptized, he, depending on his repentance, was consecrated by the Holy Spirit and was fit to preach and baptize others. It was therefore not proper that African preachers were forbidden to baptize and preside at Holy Communion because they had not been ordained or consecrated.

[22] *Livingstonia News*, Vol. 3/1 (February 1910), p. 14.

[23] Ibid.

[24] *Proceedings of the Nyasaland United Missionary Conference 1900*, p. 67.

Testament. Macalpine had earlier decided that no candidate for the catechumen's class would be recognized who did not attend school. Church contributions were demanded from candidates. In 1898, school-fees were demanded for the first time at the rate of three pence per term. The government hut tax was introduced about the same time.[25] It is no wonder then, as McCracken has observed, that the Tonga, having been roused to the peak of religious enthusiasm and eager for church membership, the key to future prosperity, found themselves confronted by a system in which it took at least two years to be admitted - and even then, by 1899, over three quarters of those applying were rejected.[26]

In this atmosphere of discontent, Kamwana created a good impression and attracted people. He said:

> I have baptized 7,000 whites in the south; I have dined with Members of Parliament. We shall build our own ships, make our own powder and make or import our own guns, etc., when the revenue is in our own hands.[27]

The colonial government's records, mission journals and oral traditions from members of the Watch Tower Movement give varying accounts of Kamwana's teachings. The colonial government described Kamwana as having "started the dissemination of seditious political and unsettling religious doctrines in the West Nyasa District"

Four points are mentioned specifically:

(1) End of taxation;
(2) Disappearance of the British rule;
(3) Final Advent in October 1914;
(4) Formation of a native state.

It is also stated that

> there is no organization nor control, native pastors are in charge of the churches and the meetings and are free to teach what they please.

---

25 *Livingstonia Report*, 1909, p. 14.
26 John K. McCracken, "The Livingstonia Mission and the origins of the Watch Tower Movement in Central Africa", unpublished paper, October 1964, p. 7.
27 McMinn, "The First Wave of Ethiopianism", p. 57.

Other points mentioned are:

(a)   the vilification of the Roman Church and British rule;
(b)   the hostility to European controlled missions and the denunciation of their doctrines.[28]

The Final Advent in October 1914 was postponed by Kamwana to between April and October 1915.

According to the Livingstonia Mission, Kamwana's movement was not apparently concerned with the instruction or elevation of the people, but confined itself to a parrot-like repetition of certain millennarian views not new to Europeans, the chief point being that Christ is to appear again (on earth) in 1914, and that only those who are found in this particular sect are to be saved, admission to which is by baptism; that the Jews are then to repeople Palestine, and then bring the end of the world. The whites were all to leave the country, and that there would be no more trouble from tax gatherers.[29] Kamwana assured his followers:

> These people, you soon will see no more for the government will go.
> In the meantime do not let your hearts be troubled; for the white men
> whom I represent will not only educate freely, but will provide
> money for taxes.[30]

Kamwana was uncompromisingly against the introduction of school fees. He told his followers:

> You are poor; the white man ought to educate you free, and give you
> books and even clothes; he ought not to take anything from you, he
> is robbing you.[31]

A sample of four Tonga people, Kamwana's followers, interviewed by the District Magistrate of the present Nkhata Bay in 1909 about Kamwana's teaching had this to say:

Philemon Keachailwa of Bandawe:

> In discussion at my house, Kamwana said to me: 'Jesus will come in
> 1914; there will be no government' This was last November.

---

[28] Malawi National Archives (MNA) C.O. 525/67, Vol. 2, 1916, pp. 189-192.
[29] "An Adventist Propaganda", *Livingstonia News*, Vol. 2/I (February 1909), p. 23.
[30] McMinn, "The First Wave of Ethiopianism", p. 58.
[31] Ibid.

Yaredi:

> Kamwana says the Lord will come soon but does not know when. There will be no judges but Christ will appoint chiefs.

Tadeyo:

> I heard Kamwana preaching that Christ would come in 1914 and that no-one would pay taxes.

Noa heard Kamwana preaching:

> Why believe the white men; they will soon go to their homes; believe the Word of God; Christ will come in 1914 and there will be no more government.[32]

When asked how Jesus would rule at Nkhata Bay and Cape Town at the same time, Kamwana said:

> Even the King we obey now is in Britain but he has got representatives ruling on his behalf.[33]

Kamwana's motto is said to have been: "to teach the people the truth and the truth to prevail, so that they should know their way".[34]

A living witness remembers Kamwana saying:

> There is no way man shall be saved by attending classes, buying baptism, but only to believe, repent and be baptised in the name of the Father, the Son and the Holy Spirit.[35]

It is clear that Kamwana, like other Russellites, preached on the four great beasts (Daniel 7:3, 17; Revelation 4:6; etc.), on the woman on the scarlet beast (Revelation 17:3), and on similar themes. When he held his first meeting at Fuwa-Chifira in October 1908, Kamwana exclaimed: "I have brought you a new message which will bring many out of Babylon."[36]

---

[32] Evidence taken by L.T. Moggridge, District Magistrate, West Nyasa, 18, 19, 20 March 1909 on the matter of the teaching of Kamwana in "Correspondence in connection with native emissaries of Mr Joseph Booth" (hereinafter "Correspondence"), Nyasaland Protectorate Legislative Council, 3rd session, 4 May 1909.

[33] Elliot Kamwana Chirwa to the Commission of Inquiry, MNA, COM 6/2/1/3.

[34] Chirwa, "Masokwa Elliot Kenan Kamwana Chirwa", p. 7.

[35] Ibid.

[36] Ibid. "Babylon" was understood to denote the state of confusion or disorder brought about by the missionaries and the colonial government.

He interpreted Russell's "Harvest" message (which I shall discuss later) to suit his own time and circumstances, such as the concrete situation of the Tonga, colonial rule, and the presence of missionaries. W. Chirwa has made a summary of Kamwana's teachings which were compiled into twenty-four or more tracts.[37] In summary, there are then three main ideas which underline Kamwana's preaching:

(i)   the promise of freedom from white rule;
(ii)   baptism which brings salvation available to everybody;
(iii)   a time of material prosperity in the Millennial Kingdom.

The Livingstonia Mission bitterly criticized the baptism administered by Kamwana. To start with, Kamwana offered a baptism which did not require a period of probation during which prospective candidates were to follow a set of prescribed lessons, but only the willingness to be baptized. A case is cited of a woman who was met in the way, running along and shouting:

> Where is Kamwana? Where is Kamwana?
>
> He is forward there; what is wrong? said one.
>
> He baptized the man that wronged me, and can he refuse me? And she ran on to be immersed.[38]

Kamwana's baptism ceremony has been described as follows:

> At baptism, the baptist joked and laughed with the people as the ceremony proceeded. The person immersed was forbidden to wring his cloth or part of it as that was to throw away the Holy Spirit, nor might he lend his cloth or part of it to another, for the same reason.[39]

Kamwana undoubtedly attracted such a large following that by March 1909, he had baptized 9,126 people.[40] He preached against the use of charms and created new methods of greeting, new burial laws and taboos, and the rejection of traditional society with its rulers. Adultery was pardoned at once by a profession of penitence. He insisted on monogamy but, on conversion, any one of the wives and not just the first married could be

---

[37] Ibid. See Appendix, pp. 25-26.
[38] McMinn, "The First Wave of Ethiopianism", p. 58.
[39] Ibid.
[40] *The Watch Tower*, Vol. XXX (1909), p. 13.

retained. By the beginning of 1909, Kamwana had made such a significant impact on his home area, Chintheche, that the administration began to take notice of him. The Resident (District Commissioner) wrote to the Deputy Governor:

> An Atonga proselyte of Mr Booth of the Zambezi Industrial Mission's fame has recently returned from South Africa after a course of religious instruction and is starting a native church and a revival in the District. He is daily making hundreds of so-called converts and baptizing same, greatly damaging the influence of Livingstonia Mission.[41]

The Resident stated further that he had heard that Kamwana was talking sedition but had not yet found the slightest evidence on this point, although he considered that "his influence in this District must prove harmful to so excitable a tribe as the Tonga".[42]

In the Livingstonia Mission circles, Kamwana's movement was noted with great concern. Fraser wrote that Kamwana

> is organising a church which seems to have a very antagonistic spirit to the established work   I fear that the movement has germs of political trouble.[43]

The information which reached Government House tended generally to point to the potential subversiveness of Kamwana's movement, given his connection or association with Joseph Booth, for a long time a threat not only to the missions but also to the colonial administration.

The Resident of Chintheche was slow and cautious to accept the verdict that Kamwana had seditious motives in his teaching.[44] However, as opposition to Kamwana was growing within the Livingstonia Mission circles,

---

[41] C.O. Ockenden, Resident, Chintheche, to Deputy Governor, Zomba, February 1909, "Correspondence".

[42] Ibid.

[43] Donald Fraser, missionary at Loudon, to the Governor, Sir Alfred Sharpe, 1 March 1909, "Correspondence"

[44] The Resident (District Commissioner) at Chintheche, L.T. Moggridge, sent a telegram to the Deputy Governor, 22 March 1909, in which he stated that he believed Kamwana to be honest in his teaching. But he noted that there were elements of danger that his followers might lose their heads. He felt that the opposition of the Mission and Kamwana's detention there would probably exaggerate his importance in the eyes of the Atonga people. See "Correspondence".

Macalpine (a Livingstonia missionary) submitted sworn evidence against Kamwana to the Government House. He added that Kamwana's teaching was dangerous and that there was widespread apprehension as to what dangerous issues such teaching might lead to.[45]

Government House was swift to take action against Kamwana and to curb his influence. In a circular issued on 27 March 1909, the Governor summarized Kamwana's case and requested all residents in the event of any 'native' entering their district and attempting, under the cloak of religion, to advance similar political doctrines, to take steps under the ordinance and report by telegram to the headquarters. Evidence was to be provided by oath. The circular went on:

> His Excellency feels that the dissemination of such doctrines as the Final Advent in the immediate future, the end of taxation, and final disappearance of Europeans should be at once stopped.[46]

Kamwana was therefore given a choice of either leaving the Protectorate or being detained at Nsanje in the extreme south of Malawi. He refused to leave the Protectorate, and consequently in March 1909 he was sent to Zomba, the seat of government, for interrogation.[47] This was to be the beginning of a long exile from his home district.

Within two days of Kamwana's arrest and his being sent to Zomba for interrogation, 9,126 of his converts or followers sent a telegram to the Governor, protesting against his being taken away from their midst. The telegram read:

> Been baptized by Elliot [;] hearing his preaching in Bible soothes our hearts [;] it gives no harm to government [;] if any complaints reached you is jealousy. Not having two churches in Livingstonia. Oh! Governor, we cry for help from you.[48]

In reply through the Resident, the Deputy Governor insisted that if, on arrival in Zomba, Kamwana could prove to His Excellency that his teach-

---

[45] "Correspondence"

[46] Governor's Circular, no. 12, 27 March 1909.

[47] Telegram, Resident, Chintheche, to Deputy Governor, Zomba, 30 March 1909, "Correspondence"

[48] Telegram from 9,126 converts, Chintheche, to Governor, Zomba, 2 April 1909, "Correspondence"

ing was innocuous and not likely to cause unrest, the Governor would have no desire to interfere with him.[49]

The Resident then called the senders of the telegram to come and see him on 3 April 1909. Five hundred from villages within eight miles of the *boma*[50] came. Their spokesman admitted the Second Advent in 1914 but said this was not insisted upon as a certainty. They all wanted a church without probation before baptism. Therefore they wanted Kamwana back, as they were not going to the Free Church.

However, in a communique to the Deputy Governor, the Resident affirmed that in his view, Kamwana should be taken away for some time. He felt that the doctrine of the Second Advent in itself was dangerous, but more so when encouraged by Booth whose loyalty was suspect. He warned that sectarian feelings would become numerous, as people wanted Christianity but not the Free Church type. Others, besides Kamwana, would probably attempt to establish their own churches. Should this independent (or quasi-religious) enthusiasm be welded into anything like a combined native church, its doings and doctrines would want careful watching, as communication with the south was constant and the chance that some attempts would be made to introduce "Ethiopian" doctrines amounted almost to a certainty.[51]

After being held up in Zomba for interrogation, Kamwana was detained in Mulanje and then sent to South Africa in June 1909. For a while he rejoined Booth in Pretoria and Durban, but towards the end of 1909, the two quarrelled over doctrinal and financial matters. Kamwana continued to be supported by the Watch Tower Movement in the USA for the period that he remained in South Africa and after he went to Chinde, probably early in 1910. There he remained for most of the next four years.

Some time in September 1910 or early 1911, Kamwana returned briefly to Chintheche to rally the Watch Tower Movement against a secessionist Seventh Day Baptist Church and also to counteract the effects which William Johnston, the WTBTS envoy from America, had upon the leaderless movement when he visited the area in September 1910.[52] He was rear-

---

[49] Telegram, Deputy Governor to Resident, Chintheche, 3 April 1909, "Correspondence"

[50] *Boma* refers to district, as well as the central administration unit in any given district.

[51] Telegram, Moggridge to Deputy Governor, 5 April 1909, "Correspondence"

[52] Cf. Langworthy, *"Africa for the African"*, p. 217.

rested and deported within a matter of days. An eye-witness has testified that an angry crowd of Watch Tower followers and sympathizers demonstrated all the way from Chintheche to Nkhata Bay until suppressed by the colonial police.

The American Seventh Day Baptists, Wilcox and Moore, visited Kamwana in Chinde in June 1912. Together with his brother, Yohane Chirwa, he had by then established a fairly large Watch Tower community there. It was said at that time that the British wanted to keep Kamwana in Chinde until the end of 1914, the year of the Parousia. At the beginning of 1914 the Portuguese put him in prison for a whole month.

In September 1914, Kamwana was allowed to return, but was detained at Mulanje until early 1916. In that year he was moved to Neno, about a hundred miles west of Blantyre. There an escape plot failed.[53] While in political detention at Mulanje, Kamwana had been corresponding with John Chilembwe, and was evidently aware that the latter contemplated some form of rising, but he refused to take any active part in it. He confessed later:

> Knowledge of the Scriptures was better than knowledge of war ...
> for knowledge is power but very few use it properly ... It was not
> for Chilembwe to wage war ... armed violence was too early.[54]

And he believed firmly that

> present powers ... will be swallowed up by war which is in process
> ... God will take vengeance on our foes, therefore I wait patiently
> for our deliverance.[55]

To the Commission of Inquiry into the Rising, Kamwana insisted that the colonial government ameliorate the conditions of the Africans:

> I submit that if possible wages should be increased. Jealousy and
> hatred of particular classes of Europeans should stop. Pension and
> allowance for the children, wife, or parents of the dead soldier in the
> war should be considered. Liberty should be given to some extent.
> Native tax collectors and policemen should stop to extort and ravish

---

[53] Pachai, "The State and the Churches", p. 14.
[54] Kamwana to the Commission of Inquiry, MNA, COM 6/2/1/3.
[55] Kamwana to Robert Elija, 12 October 1914, MNA, COM 6/2/1/3.

in the districts [sic] ... otherwise the natives would continue taking vengeance.[56]

Hence the colonial administration was unable at that time to establish any clear evidence of Kamwana's complicity in the Chilembwe Rising. However, in the aftermath of the trials which followed the Rising, Kamwana, together with William Mulagha Mwenda and his brother Yohane Chirwa, were deported to Mauritius via Durban on 27 January 1917, the beginning of the journey to the Seychelles and to twenty years of exile from his homeland.

We know very little about Kamwana's life in exile. It has been said that, while in the Seychelles, he was given an allowance of £10 per month and allowed to cultivate pineapples for sale. In June 1932 Kamwana's wife, Anna Manda, died of chronic asthma and in 1935 he arranged another marriage to Loniya Kasambara, a sister of Chief Mankhambira of Nkhata Bay. He was charged 515 rupees; 412 were for bridewealth and 100 were kept for her transport to the Seychelles where she arrived on 15 May 1936. McLuckie, the European representative of the Jehovah's Witnesses in Malawi, got in touch with Kamwana in the Seychelles and sent him the Watch Tower literature. While in detention he wrote many letters to his followers in Malawi exhorting them to accept the European representatives of the Jehovah's Witnesses, but the large majority refused.

William Mulagha Mwenda became a bitter opponent of Kamwana over the years. This is attested by two letters, both written by Mwenda himself on 19 September 1926, and obviously meant as a settlement of accounts. In the first letter he warned the churches in Malawi about Kamwana because he had deserted the Society:

> To tell you the truth, the Society regards Bro. Kamwana as their chief enemy in Nyasaland ... [but] the Society's furiousness towards Kamwana-ism is being done privately.[57]

In the second letter he denounced him to the Governor of Nyasaland as a fellow-conspirator with Chilembwe:

---

[56] Ibid.
[57] Hooker, "Witnesses and Watchtower", pp. 92, 93.

26

The serious truth is that some months before Chilembwe's rising took place, Kamwana deserted the Watch Tower and became a trusted councillor of Chilembwe, before whom Chilembwe and his collegues had no secrets.[58]

Shortly after this episode, Mwenda went over to the Church of England. He was eventually released on 10 January 1928, and went to South Africa. Another account states that he was given a job at Zomba Mental Hospital, where he eventually became insane.[59]

(iii) The Watch Tower Movement during Kamwana's Exile, 1909-1937

Malawi

The banishment of Kamwana to the Seychelles inaugurated a new era in the life of the Watch Tower Movement. In Malawi the movement suffered a temporary set-back but it began to take root in other countries such as Zimbabwe, Zambia, Zaire, and Tanzania through the influence of Malawian migrant workers.

I shall now discuss briefly how the movement fared in Malawi during Kamwana's exile and the missionary phase it had entered. The Watch Tower Movement declined after 1909 following Kamwana's arrest. Many members either went over to the Seventh Day Baptists or returned to the Free Church of Scotland. One group still opted for an independent movement. In the meantime Joseph Booth, the Watch Tower representative in South Africa, had switched over to the Seventh Day Baptist Church of the United States of America for support.[60] This resulted in the secession of most of the local Watch Tower leaders such as Gilbert Chihayi and Hanson Tandu, or (more independently) Charles Domingo, who looked to Booth and the Seventh Day Baptists to support their independent church aspirations.[61]

---

[58] R.I. Rotberg, *The Rise of Nationalism in Central Africa: The Making of Malawi and Zambia: 1873-1964*, Cambridge, Mass.: Harvard University Press, 1967, p. 69.

[59] Chirwa, "Masokwa Elliot Kenan Kamwana Chirwa", p. 16.

[60] Langworthy, *"Africa for the African"*, p. 233.

[61] J.C. Chakanza, "An Annotated List of Independent Churches in Malawi, 1900-1981", *Sources*

In 1910 Russell sent William W. Johnson of Glasgow to investigate Watch Tower missionary activity in Malawi. Johnson found a spirit of cupidity and self-seeking; people wanting him to sign employment cards to escape taxes and was jeered at when he left.[62] His report cut all the remaining links with the United States.

The Seventh Day Baptists did not make much headway either, particularly as the support from Booth was minimal. Partly due to Kamwana's brief visit and his continued letters from Chinde and the local leadership

Elliot Kamwana (second from the left) and Joseph Booth, 1909

of Jordan Msumba and Timon Chirwa, the Seventh Day Baptist pastors were ousted by their congregations in most areas of the Nkhata Bay District and there was a return to the Watch Tower.[63] The local Watch Tower congregations continued to exist independently, although with diminished strength, particularly after 1914 when the foretold millennium failed to arrive. The society was then known as the Watch Tower Churches of Christ. In August 1914 there were nearly fifty-one churches with an estimated membership of 1,000 in Nkhata Bay District and had spread south to Liwonde, Blantyre, Mulanje, as far as the Lower Shire. It had no schools,

for the Study of Religion in Malawi, no. 10 (December 1983), see item 124.

[62] Shepperson and Price, *Independent African*, p. 157.

[63] Cf. Langworthy, *"Africa for the African"*, pp. 219ff, esp. p. 244.

but Bible lessons based on the Society's tracts were taught. In the remote areas of Nkhata Bay District such as Kajirirwe, Watch Tower schools were built but ran for a short time due to lack of financial assistance. In 1914 Watch Tower pastors in Blantyre and Upper Shire District compiled the following figures for that year:[64]

Locality of headquarters	No. of meetings held	Attendance
Limbe, Southern Region	43	1,884
Linjisi, Southern Region	31	584
Ntcheu, Central Region	58	2,007

These figures show how active the Watch Tower Movement was in the Shire Highlands and in Ntcheu District in particular. It had spread from Tongaland southwards and leadership was in local hands.

In the aftermath of the Chilembwe Rising of 1915, the movement was proscribed. Members of the Watch Tower in Nkhata Bay area had remained quiet during the Rising. But in the supplementary Rising which took place at Ntcheu, the following prominent people connected with the Watch Tower were convicted of having taken a leading part in, or contributed to the Rising:

1.   Wilson Daniel Kusita: was convicted of treason and executed;
2.   Jordan Njirayafa;
3.   David Shirt Chikakuda;
4.   Yohane Elliot Chandaka Chirwa (Kamwana's brother).

In 1919 the colonial government, conscious of the danger of driving the movement underground, decided to give it a limited recognition by permitting the building of churches where the headman did not object and there were a sufficient number of followers.

The headquarters of the Watch Tower Bible and Tract Society in Cape Town once again tried to exercise control over the movement. In 1926 a white representative of the Society, H.W. Hudson, visited Malawi with his wife to investigate the state of the movement. He was so shocked by what he saw that he confessed:

---

[64] MNA, C.O. 525/67, Vol. 2, 1916, pp. 189-192. See also file SI/487/19.

The great majority of the professed native adherents have so little conception of the true meaning of the Society's doctrines and show so little promise of being either able or willing to comprehend them that he cannot accept them even provisionally as members, and though their teachings are apparently harmless, he must openly repudiate them as entirely failing in any degree to represent the Society's true tenets.[65]

In a move to restore proper order and control, Hudson appointed Richard Kalinde of Zomba as official representative.[66] But in April 1934 a permanent white representative, R.A. McLuckie, arrived in Malawi.[67] In an attempt to purge the movement, he formally disowned ninety per cent of the members.[68] These formed the Watch Tower Native Controlled while those who were not disowned, and joined McLuckie, took the name of Jehovah's Witnesses. It was to this divided Watch Tower Movement that Kamwana was to return in 1937. While in detention he wrote many letters to his followers, exhorting them to accept the European representative of the Jehovah's Witnesses and claimed the exclusive use of church property which formerly belonged to Kamwana's Watch Tower followers but, in 1936, a lawsuit in the Nkhata Bay District magistrate's court terminated in favour of the latter.[69]

The history of the remaining groups of the Kamwana Society Church which did not go over to the Seventh Day Baptists after 1909 and the history of the later newly-formed Watch Tower churches in Malawi is still unclear. The Watch Tower groups of the 1930s were indeed a manifestation of the different trends within the movement perhaps under the influ-

---

[65] Acting Chief Secretary to Provincial Commissioners, 6 July 1926.

[66] Richard Kalinde came to prominence through his membership of the Watch Tower Movement in Zimbabwe. He translated the millennial literature into Chichewa. However, he did not succeed in enjoining orthodoxy in the movement. See Cross, "The Watch Tower Movement in South Africa", p. 103.

[67] Johannes de Jager visited Malawi in 1933 as part of the general tour of Central Africa after a decision had been taken in 1931 to set the work in Africa on a more regular footing. Following the tour, McLuckie was appointed to lead the Movement. He established his headquarters in Zomba, with Kalinde as his helper. See Cross, "The Watch Tower Movement in South Africa", pp. 103-104.

[68] For example, in Karonga where John Matawale was leader of the Watch Tower and claimed a following of 783 members, he and all but ten of his followers were rejected. See Cross, "The Watch Tower Movement in South Africa", p.104.

[69] MNA, file IA/1341, "The Watch Tower".

ence of their leaders. Some of the well-known groups were: Elliot's Church, *Mpatuko* (the separated ones), *Choonadi* (Truth), and *Watch Tower wa Mzimu* (Watch Tower of the Spirit) which continued in Mzimba and other northern districts.[70]

Since the white-led Jehovah's Witnesses from 1934 onwards were canvassing, more and more members from the Watch Tower group started joining the international organization directed from Brooklyn. According to information from the Watch Tower Bible and Tract Society, when the branch office in Blantyre was opened in 1934 there were only thirty orthodox Jehovah's Witnesses in the whole of Malawi. In 1938 there were 1,065; in 1955 as many as 12,137.[71]

Zimbabwe

Sholto Cross has traced the zone of impact of the Watch Tower Movement as covering the three mining belts of settler Africa (excluding South Africa); namely, the goldfields and coalmines of Zimbabwe, the Zambian Copperbelt and the mines of the south-eastern Zaire.[72] He goes on to point out that this was a distinctive region in colonial Africa, where there was an intensive exploitation of labour, administrative control which was neither particularly penetrating or effective outside the urban areas, and only a partial mission impact.

From 1909 the Watch Tower Movement which was largely led by Tonga migrant workers, began to spread to Zimbabwe, encompassing large sections of Zambia among the Iwa, Namwanga, Mambwe, Nsenga, Lamba, and Lala in the 1920s, and in the 1930s the Copperbelt, the Luapula and valley sections of the Ila, and the Wiko peoples in Barotseland. In the mid-1930s the Watch Tower also drew support in the Katanga, and in the next two decades spread over eastern Zaire. South-west Tanzania, Mozambique and Angola were also affected by the movement.

I shall now discuss briefly the origins of the Watch Tower Movement in Zimbabwe and south-west Tanzania. Here, only the oldest Watch Tower

---

[70] Greschat, "Kitawala, the Origins, Expansion and Religious Beliefs", p. 40.

[71] Ibid., p. 42. See also M. Cole, *Jehovah's Witnesses: The New World Society*, New York: Vantage Press, 1955, p. 229.

[72] Cross, "Social History and Millennial Movements", p. 86.

groupings, such as the 'Society Church', Elliot Church and Achitawala come under the blanket term 'Watch Tower'. The missionary phase of the Watch Tower Movement in southern and east-central Africa shows how strong the membership was in Malawi. Ranger has described the Watch Tower Movement as the 'northern influence on Zimbabwean independency'.[73] It began as a religion which distributed pamphlets in 1917 and, by the late 1920s, it had extended its activity into the Shona tribal reserves. At this time it was fundamentally the faith of a Malawian elite of clerks and semi-skilled labourers. Along the Harare-Bulawayo railway line by 1923, two out of one hundred and seventy-three members were Shona, while the rest were Malawians.[74] The mining areas became centres of the movement's activities led mainly by Malawians.[75] The leader at Shamva mine was Richard Kalinde, a Malawian who was supervisor of the grain store and kitchen. He has been described as:

> thoroughly honest and reliable ... He reads a great deal and mostly books from America on the life of Christ and religious matters.[76]

It was not long before the movement fell under the government's suspicion because of its seemingly anti-European teachings. A Yao preacher at Hwange Colliery told his congregation that:

> the white people did not want natives to become clerks because they were afraid of the natives getting up in the world. There was a white man in Cape Town who would send some books and letters to him from which he would teach the natives.[77]

The Native Commissioner from Mazoe expressed the opinion in 1923 that the root cause of the movement was the spread of education of a fairly high standard in Malawi leading to a desire for control by their own people of religious matters.[78] But this did not worry the administration much so long

---

[73] Ranger, "The Early History", p. 68. See also C. van Onselen, *Chibaro: African Mine Labour in Southern Rhodesia 1900-1933*, London: Pluto Press, 1976, pp. 204-209.
[74] Ranger, "The Early History", p.70.
[75] Some of the prominent leaders from among the Malawian migrant workers were: Sadris Chirwa, Alfred Mtewa at Phoenix mine; Lameck Mwase and Richard Kalinde at Shamva mine; Gideon Banda at Eldorado mine and James Stanley Manda at Chinoi.
[76] Ranger, "The Early History", p. 70.
[77] Ibid.
[78] Ibid.

as these Watch Tower ideas did not spread to the Shona and Ndebele. In the early 1920s the administration could report:

> The church of the Watch Tower has not hitherto attempted any propaganda amongst the Mashona Natives against whom there appears to be an underlying hostility.[79]

This lenient attitude towards the movement did not last long, but soon changed into open hostility influenced mainly by the reports which came in from the Malawi and Zambian colonial governments. The Malawi authorities advised that the movement believed in:

> the destruction of all forms of government and that it was characterized by vilification of British rule and hostility to European controlled missions.[80]

A purge of the Watch Tower members followed. Known adherents were summarily deported. However this merely served to force the movement underground rather than destroying it.

As Malawi had, by 1922, lifted the ban on the Watch Tower Movement and allowed it to operate with certain restrictions and under surveillance, Zimbabwe took a similar line. A careful watch and supervision was to be exercised over the movement's activity and frequent reports rendered in this connection.

This new dispensation marked a new development in the Watch Tower Movement. Although the general feeling in 1923 was that the doctrines of the Watch Tower Movement appealed strongly to the mixed mining 'natives' and had shown no marked tendency to spread among the indigenous population, suddenly it began to spread into the countryside. By 1926 it had spread through the Logamundi District into Urungwe, Chipuriro and Chinhoyi. By 1929, thousands of people in the Zezuru and Kore-Kore Reserves had joined. As in rural Malawi, the movement posed a threat to the authority of some local chiefs. In 1929, Chief Bepura complained:

> My country is being destroyed by the Watch Tower Movement ... the movement is madness and is destroying my people.[81]

---

[79] Ibid.
[80] Ibid., p. 71.
[81] Ibid., p. 72. Quoted from files S84/A.259 and 293.

It was the Malawian preachers who spread the movement into the rural areas. When they were not at work they would organize prayer meetings in the rural areas, during which they introduced songs in their own mother tongue - Chichewa or Chinyanja - and taught about Kamwana and John Chilembwe. They would say:

> Kamwana and John Chilembwe will rise out of the water and come to the people in the *Mbuzi Moon*. They will give the people a potion to drink from a cup. This will send the recipient to sleep for seven days. When they awaken they will be white and have amassed wealth. They will not need work.[82]

The Malawi preachers, in the spirit of Kamwana, made an attack on the Shona tribal customs. In the words of the Assistant Native Commissioner of Chinhoyi:

> Their respective totems have been supplanted by the single totem of 'Israel' ... children, men, women and even mothers-in-law are shaken by all, and no modesty, as of old, is shown ... *shave* [charms] and ornaments and all the medical charms are to be discarded. People not dipped are to be shunned and referred to as *nyoka* [snake]. An Israeli cannot eat food with a *nyoka* or live close by, or come into bodily contact with one.[83]

The attack on Shona customs was not greeted with much enthusiasm in certain quarters. Chief Bepura complained:

> All our customs have been abandoned so that we elderly people who retain our old laws are apart now from those of my people who had been dipped. They are shameless in their familiarity with their mothers-in-law and they do not even salute us, their elders. They have taken European names and they say 'Our King is now America ... America is black, not white ... We shall take the white people's stores and we shall own them ... We shall be the people who remain'.[84]

As Malawian migrant workers had introduced the Watch Tower Movement into Zimbabwe in 1920s, the Shona independent churches of the spirit-type

---

82 Ibid.
83 Ibid.
84 Ibid., p. 73.

such as the *Vapostori* emerged in the 1930s. It is beyond the scope of this study to investigate possible connections between these two developments, however, it is interesting to note here that it was the Malawian migrant workers who introduced the *Vapostori* into Malawi in the early 1940s.

South-west Tanzania

The Watch Tower Movement entered south-west Tanzania in 1919 after it had been established in Malawi, Zambia, Zimbabwe and Zaire. It was introduced by Hanock Sindano, a Mambwe from Mbozi District. Sindano went to Zimbabwe in 1905 where he was initiated into the Watch Tower Movement and its teachings by five Tonga migrant workers. He heard the story of Kamwana, as the Tonga workers in Zimbabwe called themselves 'Kenanites', in honour of their exiled leader.[85]

In 1917 Sindano had become one of the leaders in the movement, and he was deported from Zimbabwe during the purge that followed. By then he had seen for himself the oppressiveness of the white system in Zimbabwe, and also the fact that the Tonga had experience of opposition to colonial government and white churches, and they were men of some education.

The return of Sindano to south-west Tanzania coincided with the confusion created by the East African Campaign and the 1918 invasion of the northern Province of Zambia by the Germans, led by von Lettow-Vorbeck. Sindano started preaching extensively in 1919. He told his followers that the colonial world was coming to an end. The authority of chiefs, administrators and missionaries was against Christ; taxes were not to be paid, and fields not to be cultivated. The faithful will purify themselves and prepare for the new order by destroying charms and protective medicines. He started constructing Watch Tower villages as new communities, or new 'Jerusalems'. He accused white men of hiding everything and teaching little about God. He said:

> they want money for what they have to give free, pay little for much hard work. Prayer will drive them back to England and make blacks as rich as they.[86]

---

[85] Ranger, "The African Churches in Tanzania", p. 14.
[86] Ibid.

Reaction from the colonial government was swift. The scale of the agitation finally prompted the local District Commissioner to use troops to arrest 138 Watch Tower adherents in January 1919. Sixty were subsequently jailed.[87] The judge's opinion in the trial was that the Watch Tower Movement made people critical of the Europeans, sceptical of their intentions and distrustful of all they did. It gave people power of self-determination against the over-government by whites and their network of rules and permits. However, it was the sudden intensification of the pressure of colonial rule and the chaos and upheavals brought by the First World War that provided a fertile ground for the adoption of Watch Tower ideas.

(iv)   Observations

The Watch Tower Movement in Zimbabwe and south-west Tanzania demonstrated its nature under urban and rural conditions. Whereas in Malawi the movement originally took root in a rural setting and developed its larger appeal in an industrial setting. When it spread abroad it first became established in an urban setting. In this industrial setting, the Watch Tower activist agitated against sub-human conditions, while in the rural setting it tended to withdraw - at least after the initial stage - into separate villages.

Can one speak of a dialectical relationship between these two settings, one influencing the other - or were the two settings simply another dimension of the urban-rural traffic? Is it possible to state that the rural Watch Tower communities were of urban inspiration above the narrowness and trivialities of traditional village life? Some aspects of urban life were brought to the rural area. Was it, perhaps, a quasi-urban setting in which returning migrants found a congenial atmosphere? Sholto Cross is of the view that the rural setting made new forms of association possible, catering for returning migrants and associated categories of frustrated and aspiring persons becoming aware of new horizons.[88] Less frequently it provided the ideological and organizational impulse for movements of defiance, rebellion and revolution.

---

[87] Sholto Cross, "Independent Churches and Independent States: the Jehovah's Witnesses in East and Central Africa", unpublished paper; see also Rotberg, *The Rise of Nationalism in Central Africa*, pp. 142-146.
[88] Cross, "The Watch Tower, Witch-cleansing and Secret Societies".

However, common to both the rural and urban forms of the Watch Tower Movements was the idea of confrontation between white and black man: hence the radicalism and anti-colonialism. Social groups with common interest were formed. In the urban setting, the movement's involvement in labour disputes was marginal in terms of direct action, but central in terms of promoting that type of consciousness which led to mass strikes and movements of hostility. Herewith a short list of strikes attributed to the influence of the Watch Tower Movement:

1923 Wankie (Hwange) in Zimbabwe: under the leadership of Alexander Mwenda and Isaac Nyasulu, associated with Elliot Kamwana.

1927 Shamva in Zimbabwe: the twenty-two leaders were all Malawians, although it is not clear whether they were members of the Watch Tower Movement, but there was a large Watch Tower membership in the mine.

1935 The Copperbelt in Zambia: despite the allegation that the Russell Commission was predisposed against the Watch Tower Movement, there was no real evidence of Watch Tower involvement.

1941 Manono tin mine in Zaire: members of the Watch Tower dressed in robes and crowns demanded justice for the workers.

Hooker mentions that the Watch Tower in Zambia after 1946 ran into conflict with the African trade unions and independence movements.[89] The opposition was in one sense that between a realistic and non-realistic interpretation of suppression and deliverance. The labour unions and independence movements believed in tackling the administration directly to bring about a new order. The Watch Tower had an attractive interpretation of who the administration was - the devil - and how its success had to be interpreted (Satan's initial victory). This was countered with the knowledge of the administration's impending downfall through divine intervention and inheritance of the goods by Africans, under a new dispensation which would reject both the African tradition and European impositions.

Sholto Cross has tried to draw parallels with E. Hobsbawm's 'labour sects' as discussed in his *Primitive Rebels*.[90] The Watch Tower appealed

---

[89] Hooker, "Witnesses and Watch Tower", p. 106.
[90] Manchester: Manchester University Press. 1959. Chapter 8.

particularly to the newest and rawest recruits in the mines, often drawn from common localities. Its millennial language both explained and offered some compensation for the discrimination and regimentation of compound life. In a variety of ways it promoted the beginnings of a proletarian consciousness.

The Watch Tower Movement began at the mines very much as a countryman's religion uniting people from the same tribe and area. In the Mashona gold field (Zimbabwe) and Kabwe coal mine (Zambia), membership was mainly composed of the Tonga from Malawi, who used the movement very much as a friendly society and a means of communication with their home country. In Katanga (Zaire), the Watch Tower was the expatriate religion of Zambian migrants, mainly Lunda and Luapula. Hence it was somewhat in the nature of an ethnic association. But the Watch Tower cannot be confined to this narrow framework. It gave knowledge of the white man's world through its leadership, and led to successful accommodation to the lot of the wage worker. Ideologically it was pan-African, with an elitist self-vision, which enabled it to broaden its base from a mere village cult.

(v)   Second Ministry, 1937-56

The second phase of Kamwana's career in Malawi began in 1937, having spent twenty-eight years in exile. When King George VI was crowned in London in May 1937, the British authorities declared an amnesty for Kamwana and Yohane Chirwa. On 13 July 1937, they boarded the S.S. Kenya which took them to Beira on their way to Malawi.

The Acting Governor ordered that they should conform to the following conditions:

a)   that they reside in their district;
b)   that they should not leave their district without prior approval of the District Commissioner concerned;
c)   that they conduct themselves at all times and in all places in the interests of peace, order and good government.[91]

---

[91]   MNA, file AI/1243, "Watchman Healing Mission".

Kamwana broke away from the Jehovah's Witnesses shortly after he had arrived in Malawi. He said that the books of the Society were good, but the Europeans were bad.[92] It would appear that Kamwana's estrangement from the Watch Tower Movement had started already while still in exile. William Mulagha Mwenda's letter written in Seychelles on 19 September 1926, warned the churches in Malawi about Kamwana because he had deserted the Society:

> To tell you the truth, the Society regards Bro. Kamwana as their chief enemy in Nyasaland ... (but) the Society's furiousness towards Kamwanaism is being done privately.[93]

It was on 16 December 1937, barely five months after returning home, that Kamwana declared he had founded another organization which he called the "Watchman Healing Mission Society". In the following year, he went on to establish the main centre for his new movement at Chiwangalumwi, to the north of Chintheche. Within a short time, Chiwangalumwi came to be regarded as the "Zion of God" from where salvation in its totality could be sought. Though primarily a healing centre, it was used also as an elementary theological institution for training preachers and as a primary school specifically for the children of the members. To show his dislike for the government and mission schools, Kamwana withdrew all his children from mission and government schools and began to teach them at home with some of his followers. But as the centre lacked financial resources as school fees had not been introduced, it was eventually closed down.

Members of the Watchman Healing Mission Society were identified by a white badge with the following words in red: *Ini wa Yehova ndi Amikaeli* meaning "Unto Jehovah and Michael" (Isaiah 44:5). As the movement grew, Kamwana came to be regarded as a prophet (*mchimi*) and the Seventh Angel (Revelation 16:17).

In his ministry he worked closely with three assistants popularly called "deacons". These were: Malijesi Phiri, a woman from Khoza Village, Lisale; Chimutika Mphande from Lisale and Robert Mnkhwakwata, short in stature, from Chidambo who also led the church's youth wing called "Amazoni". However, prominent among these three "deacons" was the

---

[92] Ibid.
[93] Hooker, "Witnesses and Watch Tower", pp. 92, 93.

woman, Malijesi Phiri, who, in her earlier life had been educated at Bandawe Mission. She preached and introduced Kamwana to the congregation at religious functions. She interpreted his exile in the Seychelles in biblical terms - as John who was taken to the Island of Patmos (Revelation 1:9). When Kamwana was on tour, visiting his congregations, she supervised the preparation of his food. Accordingly, any food or drink prepared for Kamwana had to be tasted by four different people and then only given to him after an hour had elapsed. Apparently, this was to ensure that there was no danger of food-poisoning. After Kamwana had died, some members of the church accused her of having masterminded the death, most probably through some form of poisoning, in order to assume leadership of the Church. Under these circumstances she left the Church and joined the Seventh-day Adventists where she remained until her death.

A notable event in the life of the Church during Kamwana's time was the annual one-week *misasa*[94] convention held at Lisale in sub-Chief Chinthu's village during the dry season. Some time before the beginning of the convention, the three 'deacons' went to Chiwangalumwi to be briefed by Kamwana on the manner in which the convention would be conducted. He only showed up on the last day - Saturday - for the closing ceremony. He arrived at Lisale on Friday afternoon and stayed at Chimutika Mphande's house. On Saturday at midday, the Amazoni youth assembled at the house and sang religious songs as Kamwana was getting prepared to go to the venue of the convention for the closing ceremony. After some time, Kamwana emerged, dressed in a white suit, helmet, gloves and shoes, and walked solemnly at the rear of the singing and dancing Amazoni youth procession.

Here is one procession song of the Amazoni youth:

Tumbuka	English

Refrain

Tikondwe tose kuti	Let us all rejoice
Mikaeli ndi Karonga;	Michael is Lord;
Waza pa charo	He has come into the world
Kwezyani mbendera	Lift up the banners
Ya charo cha pasi	Of the world

---

[94] *Misasa* (Chewa): These are temporal huts where people stay for a short period, in this case for the revival session.

40

Tikwezye mbendera!	Let us lift our banners!
Mikaeli ndi Karonga	Michael is Lord
Wa charo cha pasi	Of the world

When the procession finally arrived at the venue of the convention, Malijesi formally introduced Kamwana to the congregation in the following words:

| Muwonga yani | Who do you thank? |

The congregation responded:

| Tiwonga a Yehovah na Mikaeli. | We thank Jehovah and Michael. |

Then she went on:

| Asi mukuwonga a Yehovah na Mikaeli, lulutirani na kuvwina. | If you are thanking Jehovah and Michael, ululate and dance. |

In his closing sermon, Kamwana appealed to his congregation to remain united and steadfast in their faith. He insisted that Jesus Christ came into the world in 1914, unlike the Seventh-day Adventists who teach that he has still to come. On the country's political situation he said: "the whitemen you see here will go away, not far from today. Although John Chilembwe failed to liberate this country in 1915, someone else will come to liberate it". He never indicated who this person was. He cried out twice loudly: "Wake up, Nyasaland", and then went on: "all other peoples are awake, you are the only one lagging behind".

What was really new in his teaching at this latter stage of his ministry was the rejection of both traditional and western medicine and of all forms of healing except faith-healing. When a sick person was brought to him, he invoked Michael to grant the cure. For instance, for a person suffering from headache, Kamwana would pray; *"A Mikaeli nichizyeni, mutu ukupweteka"*, (Michael, heal me, my head is aching!). This invocation would be repeated by all present. After several invocations, they would all say in chorus: *"Chizyani, chizyani, Mikaeli ndi Karonga"* (Heal, heal, Michael is Lord).[95]

---

[95] Informant: Benjamin Ziba (54), Khoza Village, Lisale, 9 March 1996.

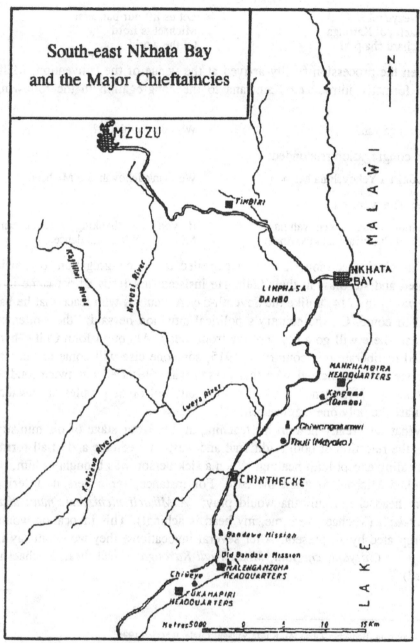

South-east Nkhata Bay
and the Major Chieftaincies

N

MZUZU

Timbiri

Rukuru River

Kavusi River

MALAŴI

NKHATA BAY

LIMPHASA
DAMBO

MANKHAMBIRA
HEADQUARTERS

Luweya River

Kangama
(Dambo)

Chiwengatumwi

Thuli (Mayoka)

Kawiuwe River

CHINTHECHE

Bandawe Mission

Old Bandawe Mission

MALENGANZOMA
HEADQUARTERS

Chiweye

FUKAMAPIRI
HEADQUARTERS

LAKE

Metres 5000   0   5   10   15 Km

Source: Department of Geography, Chancellor College, University of Malawi

When he died on 31 July 1956, the Watchman Healing Mission had 1,534 members in Malawi and 4,030 others spread throughout Zambia, Zimbabwe, South Africa and Tanzania.[96] In that year, the movement suffered a schism. Robert Mnkhwakwata, a senior member, led a secession and formed a church called Anduwila, meaning, "those who wear turbans". It is alleged that he had objected to (among other things) the dancing at prayer meetings, and to the ban on the use of medicine.

(vi)   Assessment of the Impact of Kamwana's Ministry

The main questions raised are why and how Kamwana transformed the orthodox Russellite doctrine. This is to try and find an explanation for his phenomenal success within such a short period of public ministry.

McCracken draws our attention to the retrogressive policy of the Livingstonia Mission.[97] The revivalist meetings, or 'conventions', which were started by the younger generation of missionaries in about 1895 were continued in 1902, 1904, 1906, 1911 and 1912. These sessions aroused religious fervour among the Tonga, who flocked in their large numbers to seek baptism. Macalpine reported in 1895:

> the most striking feature in the past half year ... has been the most remarkable awakening of the people around a deepened interest in the gospel message.[98]

In 1904, for example, 4,000 people attended the revivalist sessions. But by 1909 it was felt that:

> this general desire fills one with misgiving as one fears that the motive is not the best. The thing is not healthy and has its dangers.[99]

As numbers in the catechumen classes grew, the handful of European missionaries found it practically impossible to supervise the many groups spread around the area. In 1906 there were 14,000 hearers in 98 village centres. Inevitably, many candidates got frustrated as their entry into the church had either been delayed or impeded. The following table of bap-

---

[96] Chirwa, "Masokwa Elliot Kenan Kamwana Chirwa", pp. 17-18.
[97] McCracken, "The Livingstonia Mission", p. 5 and his *Politics and Christianity*, pp. 187-203.
[98] *Livingstonia Report*, January-July 1895, p. 5.
[99] *Livingstonia News*, Vol. 2/5 (October 1909), p. 68.

tisms conferred by the Livingstonia Mission in Kamwana's sphere of influence shows the situation.[100]

Ekwendeni Mission

	1905	1906	1907	1908	1909
Catechumens	651	607	94	1,058	1,124
Adult Baptisms	59	51	129	111	285
%	9.06	8.40	14.11	10.49	25.35

Loudon Mission

	1905	1906	1907	1908	1909
Catechumens	1,435	666	1,457	1,765	2,679
Adult Baptisms	87	47?	145	293	625
%	6.06	7.05	9.95	16.60	23.32

The rate of baptisms per year varied from one mission station to another depending on who the missionary in charge was. Fraser at Loudon baptized at a faster rate than his colleagues. At one time he baptized between 50% and 75% of those examined during that year. He was reprimanded by the other missionaries for this. Elmslie at Ekwendeni was on the stricter side, baptizing between 27% and 35% of the candidates per year.

The largest increase, not only for Loudon but throughout the Livingstonia Mission, occurred in 1909. This was principally due to the threat posed by Kamwana's movement. Over the next few years, the level of baptisms fluctuated considerably, dropping off from their 1909 peak in 1910.

McCracken further suggests that the strict attitude towards the conferment of baptism that the missionaries adopted was influenced by their rejection of instantaneous conversion through grace.[101] I am inclined to view this suggestion as an inaccurate rendering of Presbyterian thinking of the time. The point to be stressed here is that, according to the strict Presbyterian teaching of the day, the emphasis was on preaching and conversion first, and baptism was only a confirmation or seal of this renewal. A Livingstonia missionary could boast: "so far as the religious element was concerned it (the Kamwana movement) was no doubt a revolt against our

---

[100] McCracken, *Politics and Christianity*, p. 219.
[101] *Ibid.*, p. 187.

strict system of admission."[102] Some of the missionaries had undoubtedly become legalistic and super-cautious to a fault. Although the particular role which the Livingstonia Mission played in preparing the background for the movement is not easy to perceive, it is clear that it had something to do with creating the formal conditions for it. Kamwana found a situation in which the official religion introduced by the Livingstonia Mission was alienating hundreds of its would-be followers. Baptism was for a privileged few, an elite who were destined to benefit from the new economy introduced by the white man.

The key to Kamwana's success and popular appeal lay primarily with his interpretation of Russell's brand of millennialism. According to Russell, Christ had returned invisibly to earth in 1874, but that there would be no Kairos, no 'perfect fruit', before October 1914 - the full end of the 'Gentile Times'. The time of trouble, or 'day of wrath', which began in October, 1874 would cease about 1915. Out of this troubled time would come the Battle of Armageddon, the Millennium, the Final Judgement, and the ultimate and everlasting reign of God's Kingdom, when the forces of Evil would be defeated forever, mankind purified and made fit for the Kingdom, and those unrepentant souls who had not taken advantage of the second chance would be consigned to final, irrevocable death. Russell and his followers denounced existing churches as rejected by God, and envisaged contemporary governments as agencies of the devil.[103]

As far as I can make out, the adaptation Kamwana made to regular Watch Tower teachings lay in the interpretation of God's final Kingdom being established in Africa for the Africans, implying that Europeans did not qualify for the final election. In this new dispensation, when the black people would triumph over their oppressors, taxes, school-fees and all other forms of oppression would be abolished. It would leave the African unhindered to adopt for his own purpose those aspects of European society which attracted him most. "We shall build our own ships; make our own powder; make or import our own guns," Kamwana would cry out to his followers.[104]

---

[102] *Livingstonia News*, Vol. 3/1 (February 1910), p. 14.

[103] C.T. Russell, *Studies in Scripture IV, The Battle of Armageddon*, Brooklyn, 1897, pp. 604, 622.

[104] McMinn, "The First Wave of Ethiopianism", p. 57.

The millennium was therefore depicted as an inverted image of current secular conditions. Insofar as it sought and found connections with traditional beliefs and customs, especially witchcraft eradication, polygamy and beer-drinking, it was also a social movement aimed at the betterment of secular conditions. Furthermore, the millennium was revealed as a truth concealed by missionaries holding the key to a future reality from which they themselves were debarred. It was partly a secret knowledge reserved only for the chosen ones, in this case the black people. Ironically, Kamwana claimed to represent "white men who will not only educate freely but provide money for taxes".[105] It is not clear who these "white men" were. Could he have been thinking about the American Negroes as the militant introducers of the new age? Shepperson maintains that Kamwana promised no American Negroe or non-Christian agencies for his deliverers.[106] Alternatively it might have been simply a personalization of the coming superior power from whom he derived his own personal authority, the WTBTS.

To the original Russellite doctrine, Kamwana added the attractions of a highly apocalyptic message, centred upon the condemnation of all existing churches and governments, and the proclamation of the Final Advent in October 1914 when only those who turned to him would be saved. Russell, it must be noted, did not really argue for the end of the world in 1914-1915 (it is difficult to know exactly what he meant), but rather for the end of this dispensation: God's Kingdom would be on earth. Hans-Jürgen Greschat has written:

> It is not clear then that Russell's doctrinal system could have had no great share in Kamwana's success. In fact it seems rather to have been his criticism of the white people which was of greater fundamental significance.[107]

The author does not seem to have grasped how Kamwana interpreted the Russellite doctrine for his criticism of the white people.

---

[105] Ibid., p. 58.

[106] G.A. Shepperson, "Nyasaland and the Millennium", in Sylvia L. Thrupp (ed.), *Millennial Dreams in Action - Essays in Comparative Study*, The Hague: Mouton, 1962, p. 151. Donald Fraser said, in a letter to Sharpe dated 1 March 1909, that he had heard from native reports that Kamwana's American supporters would shortly arrive, but did not know whether black or white.

[107] Greschat, "Kitawala, the Origins, Expansion and Religious Beliefs", p. 19.

Thus Kamwana had then undoubtedly separated himself from the mainstream of the WTBTS as was testified by Johnston who, in 1910, had been sent by Russell to investigate the Watch Tower Movement in Malawi. Even his compatriot, W.M. Mwenda, denounced him in 1926 as being outside the Watch Tower orthodoxy when he secretly changed the name of the society in Malawi to Watch Tower Churches of Christ.

People who joined Kamwana's movement were mostly marginal men: non-Christians, former catechumens in the Livingstonia Mission, and church members who had revolted against the mission's strict discipline, or had been expelled from the mission. There was a nucleus of educated men, such as telegraphists, clerks, store-keepers, teachers and migrant workers.[108] It is this category of people who became propagandists of the movement in Central Africa. Through the Watch Tower Movement they felt that they could articulate their grievances while at the same time being able to feel part of a wider community.

The highlight of Kamwana's preaching was baptism, which became increasingly influenced by traditional religion and system of thought. The WTBTS tended (and still tends) to see baptism as an act of obedience signalling (but not inducing) commitment. It is not seen as having any intrinsic value or as affecting any change in the person. Kamwana, in relating it to traditional practices, may have viewed it (or his converts may have viewed it) as an almost magical agency of protection. In the style of a traditional diviner he immersed his followers so that they would acquire a special power or force - the Holy Spirit - which would not only cleanse them from sin and enroll them into the group of the elect, but also assure them immunity against evil forces, such as sorcery and witchcraft. Since the Holy Spirit was believed to become active in the baptized persons, they had just to submit in good faith to its action and wait patiently for the end of time. Whereas the Livingstonia Mission insisted on effective human effort at conversion or self-reform as a preparation for baptism, Kamwana saw this as actively induced by the Holy Spirit, perhaps influenced by Booth's type of baptism.

In Logamundi District of Zimbabwe, as Ranger has pointed out, the Watch Tower baptism degenerated into a kind of witch-finding movement

---

[108] MNA, file GOA 2/4/14 has lists of Watch Tower adherents and their jobs.

where those who did not submerge easily and completely were rejected as being unclean, or *wadunduma* - witches.[109] In south-central Zambia among the Lala and Lamba, the Watch Tower leader (Tomo Nyirenda) in the 1920s immersed people, and those who could not come up were regarded as witches. In this way he drowned over two hundred people accused of being witches.[110] But there is no hard evidence to suggest that the baptism administered by Kamwana ever degenerated into a witch-cleansing movement, despite the slanderous campaign against him by the Livingstonia missionaries.

It appears then that the appeal and the genius of Kamwana's adaptations lay primarily in the concept of the black remnant and the idea of the inverted secular society. Compared with the Shire Highlands of southern Malawi, Kamwana's sphere of influence lacked the more usual instruments of western expansion, such as settlers and heavy capital, and the main focus was on what the mission had to offer. Livingstonia, which had been founded as an industrial mission, did not have a developed millennial doctrine, apart from the traditional one of the 'Last Things'. Emphasis was on transforming the country gradually into a place where trade and industry would flourish in a Christian spirit. The mission became a great educator, employer as well as a supplier of labour for the emerging capitalist economy, not only in the Shire Highlands but also as far afield as Zambia, Zimbabwe and South Africa. Many people was regarded baptism as the key to education and a good job - in other words, to active participation in bringing about the new order.

There were two orientations, (i) gradualist and rational, which is the equivalent of post-millennial adventism, and (ii) dramatic and half-magical, the equivalent of pre-millennial adventism. That Livingstonia opted for the first may have been partly responsible for the mission's policy of making people wait for baptism. The mission looked for the more mature people who knew that they had to work and be trained to bring about a better society, and they may have rejected those who placed all their reliance on

---

[109] T.O. Ranger, "The Early History of Independency in Southern Rhodesia", *Religion in Africa*, proceedings of a seminar held in the Centre of African Studies, University of Edinburgh, 10-12 April 1964, p. 72.

[110] T.O. Ranger, "The Mwana Lesa Movement of 1925", in T.O. Ranger and John Weller (eds.), *Themes in the Christian History of Central Africa*, London: Heinemann, 1975, pp. 45-75.

baptism as a new 'magical' solution to problems. The former trained, prepared and were baptized as a sign of maturity; the latter failed to prepare, and expected supernatural intervention to produce the desired changes in them and in their social conditions.

In the eyes of many, Kamwana's baptism was a short-cut into the Scottish Mission Church, as they believed the Scots would recognize it in the same way as they accepted those who had been baptized in the industrial centres of South Africa.[111] According to his followers, the baptism did not only offer an alternative to the Livingstonia Mission's baptism, but also entitled them to the same benefits, although attained ritually rather than industrially. What really mattered to the ordinary folk, however, was that baptism offered a new sense of security through belonging to a religious community which cared for them here and now. The millennial expectations did not seem to be accepted with great certainty by the majority of Kamwana's followers. It may be that they were not the most important element in Kamwana's preaching, but at least they set a goal to his teaching.

Kamwana's biographers are silent on how the adaptation of Russell's doctrine came about. Certainly the slogan 'Africa for the Africans' came from Booth, and so did Kamwana's social concern. But Booth does not appear to have taught him this black exclusiveness. When did it arise? Could it be when the two quarrelled violently on financial matters? If this is correct, it may explain a profound dissatisfaction which expressed itself in the revolutionary change of doctrine. It is most likely to have arisen from his own life experience in South Africa which was then in the grip of 'Ethiopianism'. Having full knowledge of the situation in South Africa, Kamwana and Booth are said:

> to have commenced to carry a secret work against His Majesty's reign over the natives of Natal. They composed a treasonable document in which they clearly stated Zulu's independent Kingdom whose king then was Dinizulu.[112]

However, the plan failed because of the separation of the two shortly afterwards.

---

[111] *34th Annual Report of the Livingstonia Mission of the United Free Church of Scotland for the year 1909*, Glasgow, 1910, p. 36.
[112] William Mwenda to the Governor, MNA, 19/9/26, S2/8/26.

Kamwana appears to have been conversant with Balkan nationalism at the time. He wrote to a Watch Tower colleague:

> Did I not tell you before it happened, that Turkey will break away from the alliance with Europe and ally herself with Asia Minor? It has happened![113]

Present-day eye-witnesses still recall his sermons. He could stand up and shout emotionally, *"Kwacha Africa Yuka"* (It is dawn, Africa, arise).[114] His immediate areas of attack were taxes, education and employment, followed by an end to white authority. The Tonga still remembered mounting demonstrations in 1902, outside the district office against the increase of tax and the brutality and rudeness of Yao and Nyanja tax collectors. The King's African Rifles were called in to end the demonstration.

Kamwana's exclusivism distanced his movement from orthodox Watch Tower beliefs. According to these orthodox beliefs, the Advent and new dispensation would not be in favour of Africans alone, far from being in favour of Malawians either. In its utopian Socialism, it would be for the benefit of the oppressed regardless of their race. Moreover, the Watch Tower initially had nothing to do with Africa or the black race as such.

Elmslie, a Livingstonia missionary, put the blame on Kamwana's partial education, and then went on to say that he:

> made the religious and political elements react on each other in his work ... basically there is a revolt against the new order of things in the country.[115]

Expressing his discomfort at the movement towards autonomy among the Africans, Elmslie wrote:

> It is a symptom of a common African disease, which is at the basis of Ethiopianism. The native can jump into a white man's clothes and fancy he is the every whit as good as he, so the next step is to think that he no longer needs his presence and aid. This is a failing in the African against which missions have to battle.[116]

---

[113] Elliot Kamwana Chirwa to Yohane Chandaka Chirwa, undated, MNA, S2/6811/19.

[114] Chirwa, "Masokwa Elliot Kenan Kamwana Chirwa", p. 12.

[115] Elmslie, "Ethiopianism in Nyasaland", *Livingstonia News*, Vol. 2/5 (October 1909), p. 74.

[116] Ibid.

The promise of an inverted secular society of course has many parallels with cargo cults.[117] A new order is to come about in which there will be a reversal of roles when the weak and the oppressed will triumph. This raises several questions:

(a) the possibility of disappointment when promises are not fulfilled, particularly among the rural population;

(b) the sincerity of Kamwana and the marginal men who were too well-educated to believe such easy solutions.

Although the process of development of the Watch Tower Movement has not been studied thoroughly, in contrast to the cargo cults, the Watch Tower did persist, grow and remain an influential factor throughout Central Africa for a period of some forty years until the eve of the main nationalist movements. Several explanations may be given. The time of about five years between the beginning of the movement and the expected apocalyptic event was marked by a series of significant happenings. Malawians who were critical of European influences could appreciate the ascription of 'time of trouble' to the 1874 period, for that symbol of the European regime, the first effective Christian mission, the Free Church of Scotland's Livingstonia Mission, made its plans in 1874 and, in 1875, started work in Malawi. The First World War began in 1914 while there was already a certain amount of unrest in Malawi. The passage of Halley's comet brought hundreds of people fleeing into the bush to confess their sins and prepare for the end of the world. All these events were taken to be a partial fulfilment of the prediction. For many, especially from 1914, Kamwana then had become a *mchimi*, prophet or soothsayer. The *mchimi* then is believed to get his message from ancestral spirits. The name Kamwana itself was accorded traditional religious meaning. The Tonga have, or had, a religious concept of *Kana* or *Kamwana* (sometimes *Kananda*) *kaku Chiuta* which means 'a little child of the wonderful or Supreme Spirit'.[118] It is interesting to note that the Resident at Chintheche remarked in 1919 that the Watch Tower Movement had grown too strong

---

[117] On cargo cults, see (for instance) P.M. Worsley, *The Trumpet Shall Sound: a Study of Cargo Cults in Melanesia*, New York: Schocken, 1965.

[118] Chirwa, "Masokwa Elliot Kenan Kamwana Chirwa", p. 10.

and the believers regarded Kamwana almost as a Messiah.[119] An important point to be noted is that, whereas cargo cults were part - at best - only of oral tradition, the Watch Tower beliefs could be disseminated through literature and the better educated African could teach the educated with all the prestige of the written word-which was supplied in ever-growing quantities from the WTBTS (even if it often fed independent and schismatic movements). The WTBTS was a permanent, organized movement outside the immediate context which could, however, influence it.

The educated leadership in the mines and compounds of southern Africa could read the signs of the times as their focus was against European injustice. The Watch Tower tracts which circulated were an independent source of biblical knowledge which God had made available to Africans. Their importance lay in the discussion and interpretation of contemporary events. For those whose millennial expectations were to prove abortive in the 1914-15 period, they often sought new forms, either by changes in Watch Tower doctrine or by the assumption of new kinds of expectations, after these years had passed. In Tonga society, the *mchimi* has such a great influence that, should his prophecy fail, he or those around him were ready to offer an explanation. Admitting failure of the Advent in 1914, Kamwana said:

> It was my view as well as those of the society that the Watch Tower would be glorified ... before the end ... But by now, I, neither anybody in Europe knows how long all this will take place (sic) but that it will still happen.[120]

Kamwana's personal authority appears to derive not from his family background but rather from his being a well-travelled man. His long absence as a migrant worker in South Africa, his studies of the WTBTS doctrines under Joseph Booth and his eventual exile set him apart not only as a man who had been initiated into the mystical and superior knowledge of the world beyond, but also as a sacrificial lamb. The further afield the Watch Tower spread, the greater the mystery that surrounded his personality. Assessing Kamwana's style of preaching, the *Livingstonia News* reported:

---

[119] Chintheche Resident to Governor, undated, MNA, S2/8/26.

[120] Elliot Kamwana Chirwa to Yohane Chandaka Chirwa, undated, MNA, 52/68/19.

He was not a preacher: his style could not be described as clear, or forcible, or copious, and his influence on the people in that way was unappreciable ... But he was a strategist and struck the weak points of the situation very clearly.[121]

But his followers wrote in a telegram message: "hearing his preaching in Bible soothes our hearts".[122] It would therefore seem fair to say that Kamwana had indeed a magnetic personality which drew thousands of people to himself. He led a populist movement. The Watch Tower doctrine gave a mobilizing ideology which went beyond the political capacity of the local chiefs and headmen around Bandawe, his home area, and in Ntcheu District in the south. That is why some chiefs were against the movement from its beginning in 1908/09. The Resident at Chintheche, L.T. Moggridge, commented in 1909 that Kamwana "seems to have power of exciting emotional fervour comparable to that of revivalist England".[123]

(vii) Conclusion

The first ministry of Kamwana marked a turning point in the religious history of Malawi in its short and long-term effects. When Christianity was seen primarily as being the domain of white people who controlled all the missions, Kamwana came out to show that Africans could also play a significant part in preaching the gospel. He challenged the Livingstonia Mission's interpretation and application of the Bible to concrete needs and situations. In this way, as an initiator of religious independency, he paved the way for the upsurge of independent churches formed in the 1920s and 1930s.

McCracken has observed that "the Watch Tower had grown out of religious and social tensions rather than specifically political ones".[124] Among the Tonga, the contact with Western culture through Christianity and education created special problems of adjustment. In the struggle to attain new values introduced by Western civilization, a section of the Tonga commu-

---

121 McMinn, "The First Wave of Ethiopianism", p. 5.
122 Telegram from 9,126 converts, Chintheche, to Governor, Zomba, 2 April 1909, "Correspondence".
123 Moggridge to Deputy Governor, 22 March 1909.
124 McCracken, "The Livingstonia Mission", p. 13.

nity had been left out. As the plantation economy, with its notorious land alienation and forced labour, had not expanded to the North, and also with a small presence of the colonial administration at Chintheche, the Livingstonia Mission become the focus of Watch Tower criticism and opposition. Although the Livingstonia missionaries attacked the movement bitterly, and even influenced the colonial government to ban it, there was a move within the Livingstonia Mission circles to respond favourably to some of the Watch Tower grievances. This was seen particularly in the gradual devolution of power and authority into local hands. The first three African ministers, Yesaya Zerenji Mwasi, Hezekia Twea, Yaphet Mponda Mkandawire, were ordained in 1914. Mwasi was stationed at Sanga, a Watch Tower stronghold, in order to counteract its influence. It would appear also that the very strict regulations regarding the catechumenate were relaxed as there was a marked rise in the number of baptisms in the whole Livingstonia Mission in 1909 - an increase of almost 128% compared to 1908.

On the political scene, the Watch Tower Movement shaped the balance of power and determined the religious map of Tongaland. McCracken has suggested, although with uncertainty, that the Watch Tower gained ground in the periphery of the Livingstonia Mission's influence and accounts for this fact on the grounds of the denial of mission benefits to those remote areas.[125] But W. Chirwa does not see the denial of mission benefits as the central issue.[126] He has shown how the Watch Tower Movement was used to settle old rivalries. In south Chintheche, Chief Marengamzoma had superseded the original owner of the land, Chief Chiweyo, as he had hosted the missionaries and the colonial government officials. To boost his own influence and counteract that of Marenganzoma, Chiweyo played host to Kamwana and the Watch Tower Movement.

In north Chintheche, Chief Mankhambira had superseded Chief Kang'o-ma, the original owner of the land, through extensive trade links and use of guns. Kango'ma then sought patronage of the mission and the colonial government to oust Mankhambira from power. Mankhambira, however, eventually got baptized in the Watch Tower. Such conflicts and rivalries were

---

[125] McCracken, *Politics and Christianity*, p. 202.
[126] Chirwa, "Masokwa Elliot Kenan Kamwana Chirwa", pp. 19-20.

known to have existed even at a lower level among village headmen. Each sought to join one or another religious organization which could legitimatize his authority and position. The Watch Tower strongholds, Chifira and Sanga, became so rapidly anti-white that they were later declared 'unvisitable by whites, missionary or colonial'. Thus, as the number of independent churches grew, Tonga society split into rival and, at times, antagonistic groups along local church affiliations. However, individual members usually enjoyed a high degree of identity and togetherness which even cut across kinship ties.

Among the Maseko Ngoni of Ntcheu, the Watch Tower - as Ian and Jane Linden have suggested - quickly gained ground because it addressed itself to the hardships which they had been suffering at the hands of the British. The colonial government had divided their land by creating international boundaries so that one part became Portuguese. Worse still, the British had shot dead the Ngoni paramount chief and had refused to give official government recognition to his heir.[127]

Therefore, in rural Malawi, the attraction of the Watch Tower Movement has also to be seen in terms of political options, which were dictated by the circumstances of the time and place, as the Nkhata Bay and Ntcheu contexts have shown.

The detention of Kamwana in the Seychelles for twenty-seven years was a period of trial of strength for the movement. Many prominent leaders left and joined other churches, especially in the aftermath of Kamwana's arrest. Nonetheless, the movement entered a missionary phase not only abroad but also at home. The few local leaders who had remained faithful to the movement spread it to the southern districts and formed groups with differing trends. The abortive attempt at external control by the parent organization in South Africa ended with the introduction of a rival white-controlled movement.

Understandably, when Kamwana returned home from exile, he was militantly against the Jehovah's Witnesses and, to a lesser extent, the colonial administration. Much as one would have expected him to be received as a

---

[127] Ian and Jane Linden, "Chiefs and pastors in the Ntcheu Rising of 1915", in R.J. MacDonald (ed.), *From Nyasaland to Malawi: Studies in Colonial History*, Nairobi: East African Publishing House, 1975, p. 171.

hero and wield even more influence than before, he had come to a much weakened movement due to internal strife, divisions coupled with the rapidly growing rival organizations. Kamwana's militancy against the Jehovah's Witnesses is reflected in the following communication. On 3 March 1947, the branch office in Blantyre wrote to Kamwana:

It has come to our notice that you have been leading the people to believe you are in co-operation with the Watch Tower Bible and Tract Society of Brooklyn, New York, America, and that you receive correspondence from the President of the Society ... Very good! We ... suggest that all of us ... meet together before the public ... if you refuse to meet us and explain your claim of authority and power ... then all the people will know that you have no grounds for such a claim.[128]

On 7 March 1947, Kamwana replied:

The Watchman Mission has no time to waste on rumour, because the Blacks and the Europeans in Nyasaland know that the Watchman Mission is separate and distinct from the Watch Tower Bible and Tract Society of Europeans. The Watchman Mission represents the Healing Prince Jehovah, the Healing Prince Michael, the Kingdom of Righteousness. The power of man to fear Jehovah comes from heaven, not from Brooklyn of America or elsewhere. Hating and arguing with one another is of no assistance for such destroys the work of righteousness.[129]

Therefore the long exile does not seen to have made Kamwana less critical of the mission and government. According to a Police report of 1940, it was publicly proclaimed in his church, among other things:

If we obey the laws on earth made by the *boma*, then we are wor-shipping the devil ... People must not be afraid to break government laws. Nobody should remove his hat to the Provincial Commissioner or the District Commissioner. These gentlemen ... are pretenders.[130]

In the meantime there had been new developments on the local scene. The Native Associations formed in the 1920s and the Nyasaland African

---

[128] Greschat, "Kitawala, the Origins, Expansion and Religious Beliefs", p. 41.
[129] Ibid.
[130] MNA, file IA/1341.1.

56

Congress formed in the early 1940s had become the institutional means of articulating the people's grievances to the colonial administration. Besides, eight other independent churches had already started in his area so that he was no longer the only centre of attraction as a church leader. Nevertheless, his personal skills as an organizer still gained him respect, not only at home, but also in the neighbouring countries where the Watchman Healing Mission had a presence. Indeed, his later foundations were churches, rather than movements.

But, as he grew older, he chose to concentrate on religious activities rather than the merely political concerns. Chiwangalumwi as a 'Holy City' became a symbol of his withdrawal from secular society in order to establish a new identity for his church, as well as for himself.

Part II: Wilfrid Gudu and the Ana a Mulungu

(i) Introduction

The Ana a Mulungu church which today has small communities in Thyolo, Mulanje, Machinga, Ntcheu and Mwanza Districts, was founded in Thyolo District by Wilfrid Gudu in 1935.[1] It is particularly noted for its conscientious objection to hut tax and soil conservation policies during the colonial period. In the history of religious independency in Malawi, the Ana a Mulungu ("Children of God") are unique in their attempt to form a total religious institution with a form of communal life unknown in other churches.

A total institution, according to Erving Goffman, may be defined as a place of residence and work where a large number of like-situated individuals, cut off from the wider society for an appreciable period of time, together lead an enclosed, formally administered round of life.[2] Goffman singles out four common features of total institutions, which are:

a) All aspects of life are conducted in the same place and under the same single authority.

b) Each phase of the member's daily activity is carried on in the immediate company of a large batch of others, all of whom are treated alike and are required to do the same thing together.

c) All phases of the day's activities are tightly scheduled, with one activity leading at a pre-arranged time into the next, the whole sequence of activities being imposed from above by a system of explicit formal rulings and a body of officials.

---

[1] On Wilfrid Gudu and the Ana a Mulungu, see Rotberg, *The Rise of Nationalism in Central Africa*, pp. 151-155; MNA, file IA/1341 and IA/1413; *Annual Reports of the Provincial Commissioners for the year ended 31 December 1938*, Zomba: Government Printer, 1939; Albert Kambuwa, "Malawi: Ancient and Modern History", unpublished manuscript, Zomba: University of Malawi Library, n.d.; R.B. Boeder, "Wilfred Good and the Ana a Mulungu", History seminar paper, no. 3, Chancellor College, University of Malawi, 1981-1982.

[2] Erving Goffman, *Asylums: Essays on the Social Situation of Mental Patients and Other Inmates*, New York: Anchor Books, 1961, p. xiii.

d)	The various enforced activities are brought together into a single rational plan purportedly designed to fulfill the official institution.[3]

In the study of new religious movements, however, Harold Turner has come up with a typology of social forms under which a total religious institution is referred to as a 'total community'. Such communities are called 'New Jerusalem', 'Holy City', or 'Zion'.[4]

Adrian Hastings has described holy cities as: "permanent human communities specifically ordered according to a cycle of prayer and ritual."[5]

In this case study I shall discuss the career of Wilfrid Gudu (often spelt Good), first in the Seventh-day Adventist Mission more commonly known as Malamulo Mission in Thyolo District, and secondly as founder and leader of the Ana a Mulungu till his death on 14 March 1963. I shall raise in particular the following questions:

(a)	What are the characteristic elements of this unique style of religious independence?

(b)	Why did this new style become effective in the Thyolo District and at that particular time?

## (ii)	Thyolo District in the 1930s

I will begin by setting the scene in Thyolo District as it was in the mid-1930s.

The Mang'anja people, a sub-group of the Chewa, are Thyolo's autochthonous population. It was only from the 1890s that small bands of the Ngoni from the Central Region, large groups of Lomwe sub-groups, and other groups such as the Yao, Chikunda began to migrate to Thyolo District.[6] At the census of April 1931, the following ethnic groups were recorded in Thyolo District:[7]

---

[3] *Ibid.*, p. 6.
[4] H.W. Turner, *Religious Innovation in Africa: Collected Essays on New Religious Movements*, Boston: G.K. Hall and Co., 1979.
[5] Adrian Hastings, *A History of African Christianity, 1950-57*, London: Cambridge University Press, 1979, p. 78.
[6] On immigrations into Thyolo District, see M. Tew, *Peoples of the Lake Nyasa Region*, London: Oxford University Press, 1950, pp. 4, 30, 34, 98.
[7] *Nyasaland Protectorate Annual Report upon Native Affairs*, 1931, Appendix "A", p. 67.

Chewa/Chipeta	50
Ngoni	4,461
Yao	3,085
Nyanja/Mang'anja	14,152
Lomwe	37,116
Chikunda	273
Others	20
Total	59,154

There were six chiefdoms, four were Mang'anja, one was Ngoni, and one Kololo. The Lomwe immigrants, who were in the majority, were represented by only a handful of councillors.[8]

An influx of Europeans came into the district after the First World War, who bought or leased huge tracts of land for agriculture from the British Central Africa Company and the British East Africa Company. The Africans living on the land which had been sold or leased were reduced to the status of tenants. The tenant system was that Africans living on the land were compelled to work for the estates. No money for rent was accepted. Africans had to work one month in the wet season for rent and another month for hut tax, that is two months work. A month was reckoned at twenty-eight days actual work, and by various devices, the Africans were compelled to work considerably longer periods, e.g., if a person did not complete his day's task, no credit was given to him for the time he had worked, and occasionally he had to work several days extra to make up for the day lost. Failure to comply with these regulations could end up in eviction from the land. This tenant system which stipulated compulsory working for the landlord in lieu of paying rent, is locally known as *thangata*, which means 'help'.[9] Statistics from the 1930s show that at least 65% of the land in central and northern Thyolo had either been sold or leased. It was reported in 1935 that "in Thyolo District, 76% of the villages con-

---

[8] On the early Lomwe immigrations, see Thomas Galligan, "The Nguru Penetration into Nyasaland, 1892-1914", MacDonald (ed.), *From Nyasaland to Malawi*.

[9] For a general discussion of *thangata* in Malawi, see J.A.K. Kandawire, *Thangata: Forced Labour or Reciprocal Assistance*, Zomba: Research and Publications Committee of the University of Malawi, 1979, and Bridglal Pachai, *Land and Politics in Malawi, 1875-1975*, Kingston, Ontario,: Limestone Press, 1978. On how *thangata* worked in Thyolo District, see C.Z. Chidzero, "Thangata in Northern Thyolo District: A Socio-economic Study in Chimaliro and Bvumbwe Area", History seminar paper, no. 13, Chancellor College, University of Malawi, 1980-1981.

taining 57% of the total native population are on privately owned land".[10]
The remaining part was crown land where about half the population resided
at the rate of 136.5 per square mile, being one of the highest population
densities in the whole country.[11]

The following table shows the population increase in Thyolo District
between 1934 and 1939:[12]

Year	Population	Density per square mile
1934	66,131	105.98
1935	70,001	127.27
1936	71,979	130.09
1937	84,912	136.07
1938	89,992	144.02
1939	93,120	149.02

This steady population growth had adverse effects on people's normal
lives. A report published in 1939 reads.

> The Thyolo District is rapidly acquiring an unenviable reputation for
> crime: larceny, burglary and house-breaking are all too frequent.[13]

The Europeans tried with little success to grow tobacco, cotton and sisal.
However, during the Great Depression, they started to grow tea. This
proved a great success so that, by 1937, large expanses of land were
already under cultivation. For the Africans, this meant either moving to the
already over-crowded crown land in search of gardens, or reliance on their
low wage employment for most of their needs.[14] Those who settled on
crown land could grow enough maize and beans to feed themselves and sell
the surplus to the labourers on the estates and other places. The cash

---

[10] *Annual Report of the Provincial Commissioner for the year ended December, 1935*, p. 11.

[11] *Cholo District Annual Report for 1937*, MNA, file no. NSE 5/1/5.

[12] Compiled from the *Annual Reports of the Provincial Commissioners for the year ended: 1934, 1935, 1936, 1937, 1938, and 1939.*

[13] Ibid., 1939, p. 37.

[14] Boeder, "Wilfred Good and the Ana a Mulungu", p. 3, gives the following details: Wages for 1938 were:
a) for unskilled weeders and hoers on tea estates: nine shillings plus six or nine pence as food money (*phoso*).
b) for average tea plucker: fifteen shillings to twenty shillings per month.
c) for skilled plucker: thirty shillings plus food money.

earned from these sales could be used for paying taxes and buying essentials.

A tea plantation in Thyolo District

In the 1930s, there were at least ten religious denominations represented in Thyolo. Five were Independent African Churches and the other five were European-led missions. The missions were: Seventh Day Baptist (SDB), Nyasa Industrial Mission (NIM), Seventh-day Adventist (SDA), Roman Catholic (RC), and the Church of Central Africa Presbyterian (CCAP). The three largest among these were:

I   The RC, with eighty-six primary schools and eight outstations;
II   NIM, with fifty-four primary schools and twenty-two prayer houses;
III   SDA, with thirty-eight primary schools and twenty-eight prayer houses.[15]

---

[15] *Cholo District, Annual Report for 1937.*

It is in the context of the SDA that the career of Wilfrid Gudu and his Ana a Mulungu church will be placed.

(iii) Wilfrid Gudu and the Malamulo SDA Mission

The early life of Wilfrid Gudu has not yet been properly investigated. The little we know is that he was a Mang'anja, born probably in the late 1880s at Machiringa Village (some sources say Chaoneka Village) in the area of Village Headman Khwethemule near Malamulo Mission in Thyolo District.[16] He went to Malamulo Mission Primary School in 1906, where among his teachers were the pioneer Black American missionaries, Thomas Branch and Joel Rogers, and Malawians such as Phillip Masonga and Simon Ngaiyaye.[17] When, in 1911, Gudu became a full church member, he was given a teaching post in the mission's primary schools. In 1918, while teaching at Msomela Village school at Malabvi near Limbe, he is said to have become mentally ill for a while, and spent several weeks wandering naked in the bush. This episode has been cast in a prophetic narrative by his followers, who have provided me with the following detail:

> In 1934, Gudu was caught by the spirit of Jehovah. He retired to the bush where he spent four days in prayer, without taking any food. Snakes came near him but did not bite him. People, however, said that he was mad when in fact he was being taught another way of worship, names of the months and times. He was instructed to call his church *Ana a Mulungu*.[18]

Three years later Gudu was transferred to another SDA school at Matandani, near Neno. There he unsuccessfully tried in 1922 to rally the

---

16 "The Historical Survey of Native Controlled Churches Operating in Nyasaland", 1940, compiled by M.C. Hoole for Police Records, MNA, file no. IA/1341.

17 The Malamulo Seventh-day Adventist Mission was established in 1902 by Joseph Booth on 3,000 acres at Plainfield in Southern Thyolo District. In 1904, Booth separated from the Adventists and in 1907 the mission became known as Malamulo. See V.E. Robinson, "History of the South-East African Union", unpublished typescript, South East Africa Union of Seventh-day Adventists, Blantyre, 1952. See also Cedrick K. Khanje, "Impact of Malamulo Mission in Southern Thyolo 1902-1972: A Broad Perspective", History seminar paper, no. 3, Chancellor College, University of Malawi, 1972-1973.

18 Account written for J.C. Chakanza by Pastor Samson Chilembwe [74] "Zion: Ana a Mulungu", Molere, P.O. Makwasa, 15 September 1984. It is an extract from the Ana a Mulungu's manuscript entitled "*Masomphenya a Gudu*" (The Revelations of Gudu). Note the change of date from 1918 to 1934.

Mang'anja group against the Ngoni who held prominent positions in the Mission, though foreigners or late-comers to the area.

The SDA missionaries did not allow African teachers to wear shoes and hats in public as their non-African counterparts did. Gudu bitterly criticised this ruling in 1925, and in retaliation the authorities demoted him from teacher to carpenter. Thereupon, Gudu approached his uncle, Village Headman Khwethemule and asked for a place where he could settle and build a house. He was given a place at Molere in Kaponda's village, Chief Ntondeza, twelve miles south of Malamulo Mission. By 1926, Gudu had already built a brick house, and settled in it. He became a carpenter and part-time preacher for the next nine years.[19] Matters came to a head in 1935 when Gudu ran into conflict with the mission authorities once more. Describing the incident, he wrote:

> There was a case of adultery at Malamulo. I said publicly that it ought to be settled with justice, against the boy responsible. He was not suspended, but I was, because of what I had said. I told the Mission that I would not attend Holy Communion until six months had passed. After about five months the Mission wrote saying I was no longer a member. I asked what I had done. I was told I had been dismissed because of my disagreement with adultery.[20]

In fact, the Mission suspended him from church membership for five months for his interference in the adultery case. Later, Pastor G.R. Nash told him formally that he was no longer a member of the Seventh-day Adventist Church on this count, and also because of his failure to pay church tax during the period of his suspension.

Gudu saw this action as an anti-Mang'anja campaign organized by the Ngoni, and accused them of advising the missionaries badly. He said:

> The Seventh-day Adventists have no righteous judgment because they are leaving evil people as pastors; therefore ... [I] cannot stay with them and partake of the Lord's Communion officiated by such evil men.[21]

---

[19] MNA, file no. IA/1341.

[20] Rotberg, *The Rise of Nationalism in Central Africa*, p. 152.

[21] *Ibid.*, character portrait of Wilfrid Gudu by Pastor James Ngaiyaye, 27 February 1938.

He then demanded a remuneration of £175-10-0 for his services as a prayer house leader during the previous nine years, but the Mission simply ignored his claims.

(iv) *Zion ya Yehovah*

Following his separation from the Seventh-day Adventist Church, Gudu contemplated starting a new church. According to Kambuwa, God instructed Gudu in a vision to feed his flock at Molere:

> Wilfrid, God the Lord has blessed you. He wants you to teach His people about the truth of God which I am going to tell you now. You must observe the Sabbath as a Holy Day and teach other people to make similar observation like Moses did to the People of Israel.[22]

Accordingly, Gudu paid a visit to the District Commissioner for Thyolo, W.D. Phillips, and asked how he was supposed to teach his children, now that he was dissociated from the Seventh-day Adventist Church. Gudu used the word 'children' figuratively to mean his own followers, but Phillips took it literally and suggested that he (Gudu) teach them himself. A contemporary of Gudu has given me the following information on this issue:

> Gudu was caught by the Spirit and he said to the Missionaries at Malamulo: 'I have worked for you for nine years but without pay. Therefore you are unjust. I insist that you give me my whole pay. If you don't, I shall resign from your service and then start my own church'. As the Missionaries had refused to give him any payment for his work, he brought the matter to the District Commissioner who ruled out that Gudu should be allowed to start his church.[23]

In that year (1935) Gudu started a church which he called Ana a Mulungu (Children of God). The name of the church was taken from Matthew 5:9, "Blessed are the peacemakers, for they shall be called children of God".[24] At Kaponda Village he founded a quasi-religious community, which he

---

[22] Kambuwa, "Malawi: Ancient and Modern History", p. 9.

[23] Samson Chilembwe, "*Masomphenya a Gudu*".

[24] Report on Wilfred Good by Thyolo District Commissioner, D.M. Martin dated 29 July 1941, MNA, file no. IA/1413. However, while others refer to I John 3:1. Gudu's contemporaries insist that the name of the church was revealed to Gudu by God.

called *Zion ya Yehovah* (Jehovah's Zion). He attracted a number of followers from the neighbouring villages and, by 1939, about sixty people had
each built a house in neat lines around two sides of a small hill, topped by
his own house. The attraction of the village lay in its unique combination
of industrial activity and religious piety. Agriculture, carpentry, tailoring,
shoe-making, basket-making, pottery, cloth-weaving and building were
among the many engagements which kept the people busy. Gudu's successor has described the day-to-day life and activities of the *Zion ya Yehovah*
community, as follows:

> The normal day starts with morning prayer in our *kachisi*[25] which is
> a circular area surrounded by a reed fence with a roofed pulpit in the
> centre. There are wooden benches for the worshippers, placed in a
> semi-circle round the pulpit. When entering the sacred enclosure we
> remove our shoes, as Jesus never allowed anyone wearing shoes to
> speak to him. We also make sure that we do not have any money in
> our pockets, as the word of God is not for sale. We do not close our
> eyes when praying. At the end of the service we clap our hands.
>
> After prayer, we disperse, and each person goes to do the job
> assigned to him by the community. We work usually in teams. For
> instance, some men go to fetch building materials for our houses,
> maize-bins, kraals, etc., while others make hoe handles, wooden
> plates, furniture, baskets, weave cloth, etc. Some women go to fetch
> clay for making pots while others smear the floors and walls of our
> houses with moist earth. There is also a communal garden which we
> all cultivate. The produce is shared among all the families according
> to their needs. During the day, children attend an elementary school
> which belongs to the community. At noon, work stops and everyone
> returns home for lunch.
>
> After lunch, at about 2.00 pm, someone sounds a call to prayers by
> shouting 'Time! Time! Time!' instead of ringing a bell. After prayer
> we retire to our houses for private jobs. At sunset we gather for
> another prayer session which at times consists of psalm singing while
> members march three times round the *kachisi*.[26]

---

[25] Hut or enclosure for offering prayer and sacrifice.
[26] Account written for J.C. Chakanza by Gidioni Stivini [82], successor of W. Gudu, Mulonda Village, T.A. Nsambwe, Thyolo, 15 September 1984.

People who join the *Zion ya Yehovah* are not baptized but only have hands laid on them by the pastor. Children also have hands laid on them and are given a blessing. Seeking employment outside the community is not permitted. Members wear white uniforms. Serious offences are not pardoned. Gudu maintained that they have already been recorded by God and therefore they cannot be forgiven. For instance, pregnancy outside wedlock is regarded as a serious offence. The culprits, together with their parents, are permanently removed from the community. People who commit minor offences are sometimes suspended for a few days, during which they have to leave *Zion ya Yehovah*.

Gudu is believed to have received a revelation from God (*Masomphenya a Gudu*) which urged him to adopt the names of months found in the Bible. The following table shows the Ana a Mulungu's reckoning of months:[27]

Month	Gregorian calendar	Gudu's calendar		Biblical references
1	January	Abibu	[Abib]	Exodus 13:4
2	February	Zifi	[Ziv]	1 Kings 6:1-3
3	March	Sivani	[Sivan]	Esther 8:9
4	April	Tamusi	[Tammuz]	Ezekiel 1:1
5	May	Ata	[Ab]	Ezra 7:9, Ezekiel 20:1
6	June	Eluli	[Elul]	Nehemiah 6:15
7	July	Etanimu	[Ethanim]	1 Kings 8:2
8	August	Buli	[Bul]	1 Kings 6:38
9	September	Kisilevi	[Chislev]	Zechariah 7:1 --
10	October	Tebeti	[Tebeth]	Esther 2:16
11	November	Segati	[Shebat]	Zechariah 1:7
12	December	Adara	[Adar]	Esther 9:1

Although Gudu modelled his biblical calendar on the Gregorian one, it is worth noting at this point that the Jews had another mode of reckoning which took into account the facts of physical geography and the seasons

---

27 Information provided by Willison Mulepa [67], Ana a Mulungu, Kuweruza Village, T.A. Changata, Thyolo, 15 September 1984.

fixed for the various annual feasts. They had two years, the sacred and the civil. The sacred began in March or April (according to the moon), the month of deliverance of the children of Isreal from Egypt, and the civil in September or October, the commencement of the planting season. The prophets used the former; those engaged in civil and agricultural concerns, the latter. The year was divided into twelve lunar months, with about every third year a thirteenth. The first month of the sacred year was the one whose full moon followed next after the vernal equinox, and therefore was sometimes called March and sometimes April and sometimes parts of both. Till the return from captivity, these months had no separate name, except the first, which was called Abib (the month of 'the green ears of corn'), or Nisan, the month of 'the flight'.

He also introduced another way of reckoning days. The twenty-four hour day is equivalent to two days (John 11:9, Daniel 7:25). The first day starts at 6.00 am and ends at 5.00 pm; the second day starts at 6.00 pm and ends at 5.00 am. Below is an illustration of how the Ana a Mulungu reckon their twelve-hour day:[28]

Twelve Hour: Day One		*Twelve Hour: Day Two*	
6.00 am	1st hour	6.00 pm	1st hour
7.00 am	2nd hour	7.00 pm	2nd hour
8.00 am	3rd hour	8.00 pm	3rd hour
9.00 am	4th hour	9.00 pm	4th hour
10.00 am	5th hour	10.00 pm	5th hour
11.00 am	6th hour	11.00 pm	6th hour
12.00 noon	7th hour	12.00 midnight	7th hour
1.00 pm	8th hour	1.00 am	8th hour
2.00 pm	9th hour	2.00 am	9th hour
3.00 pm	10th hour	3.00 am	10th hour
4.00 pm	11th hour	4.00 am	11th hour
5.00 pm	12th hour	5.00 am	12th hour

It is appropriate to observe here that the natural day for the Jews was from sunrise to sunset (as with the Romans), and was divided (after the Captiv-

---

[28] Information provided by Nyado Suluma [16], Mafunga Village. T.A. Changata, Thyolo.

ity) into twelve hours of unequal length. The civil day (the day used in common reckoning) was from six in the evening to six the next day; differing in this respect from the Roman civil day, which, like ours, was from midnight to midnight. This was divided again into day and night of equal length. The day, properly so called (from six in the morning till six at night), was divided into twelve hours, of which the third, the sixth and the ninth were devoted to public services of worship. The Ana a Mulungu held communal prayer meetings three times a day, in the morning, at noon and in the evening.

(v)   Wilfrid Gudu in Conflict: The Maize Garden Issue

Gudu's appearance was impressive. He was about six feet tall, well-built and with a light complexion. He spoke very forcefully with a Ngoni/Chewa accent which he had picked up when he worked with the Ngoni at Malamulo Mission. His face usually looked so serious that when he spoke he appeared as if he were scolding someone. He wore a white collarless shirt called *mwinjiro* reaching just above the knees, and a pair of white trousers which were sewn by hand and not by machine. He wore two large wooden keys around his neck, one for opening the gates of bondage here on earth, and the other for the portals of heaven. He was often seen wearing a white helmet (some say a white cap, called *chikofiya*) and locally-made sandals.[29]

During services, Gudu and his male followers wore white surplices. When he preached, he stood in the pulpit while his congregation sat on the benches. He often spoke with a guttural sound which elicited emotional responses. Essentially, he felt he had a divine call to be leader of an oppressed people. Kambuwa has described his conviction:

> Gudu's message to the people was that he was the only man who had the true Gospel from God, and that all the other churches failed to perform God's will correctly. They were preaching about the second coming of Jesus Christ and were telling people to repent when they themselves were sinners. Gudu stated that he was the true preacher who was asked by God to preach His word. He said that because God the Lord had sent him to save the people from their sins, he

---

[29] Information from Gidion Stivin and also Perigo Williams Phiri [15] with Willie Kasonga, Mafunga Village, T.A. Changata, Thyolo.

[Gudu] was Jesus Christ No. 2, because the term 'Jesus' meant one who saved people from sins.[30]

Even early in his career Gudu was critical of the missions and the colonial administration as is reflected in this excerpt from a 1944 sermon at Nsanje:

> The Europeans came with the word of God but they were selling it with money. When a child goes to school they are charged school fees, that is why I say they are selling the word of God.[31]

Gudu's religious convictions had become more outspoken when his plan of engaging in farming to make his *Zion ya Yehovah* self-reliant ran counter to the regulations of the local chiefs and the colonial government.

The people who had come to settle at *Zion ya Yehovah* had left their villages without the permission of their village headmen, nor did they - in accordance with local custom - seek Kaponda's permission to reside in his area. Soon after, the village headmen concerned began to complain about their people's movements. As numbers grew at the *Zion ya Jehovah*, the scarcity of land became acute. Gudu planned to raise enough money to pay his men's hut taxes for 1937, and therefore resorted to growing maize in the surrounding area. Accordingly, he and his followers planted maize in late 1936 in an area which he claimed to have been given by Village Headman Khwethemule in 1925 to graze his two head of cattle which had died in 1935. This land had in the meantime been cultivated by seven people who had not become members of the Ana a Mulungu church. When these men found out that their gardens had been taken over by Gudu and his followers, they protested vigorously to Village Headman Kaponda, Chief Ntondeza and Major Pegler, the District Commissioner for Thyolo.During the three separate hearings of the case, Gudu asserted that he had been given a square mile of land by Village Headman Khwethemule (who had since died) on which to graze his two heads of cattle. As the land belonged to him, he had the right to allow his followers to cultivate it. Ntondeza and Kaponda disputed this claim, since Gudu could not produce any evidence of the arrangement with Khwethemule. Gudu assumed a truculent attitude towards Ntondeza and refused to pay attention to any recognized authority.

---

[30] Kambuwa, "Malawi: Ancient and Modern History".
[31] Reports on Native Controlled Missions, Quarterly Reports 1 and 2/44, MNA, file no. IA/1339.

A maize garden being washed away by torrential rain.
Bunding was considered to be a remedy for soil erosion.

Pegler ordered the return of these gardens to their original owners, since Gudu had no title or claim to the land in dispute.[32] Gudu, still adamant, appealed for redress to the Senior Provincial Commissioner in Blantyre, J.C. Abraham. Abraham tried to dissuade him from resisting the colonial administration, but to no avail. The original owners of the garden reaped the harvest and gave a portion to the Ana a Mulungu, but he refused to take it.[33]

It has been recounted that on one night thereafter, God came to him in a dream and told him it was time to separate from the Europeans, that Wilfrid Gudu was now the government. Taxpayers were the Sons of Evil; non-taxpayers the Sons of God. Since the government had stolen his means of paying taxes, Gudu decided not to pay them at all.[34]

Thereafter, Gudu developed an attitude of non-cooperation with the administration. He refused to supply the information required under the

---

[32] Record of hearing of the case of Wildfred Good, MNA, file no. IA/1341; Boeder, "Wilfred Good and the Ana a Mulungu".
[33] Gidioni Stivini and others do not mention that those who reaped the harvest ever gave part of it to the Ana a Mulungu.
[34] Kambuwa, "Malawi: Ancient and Modern History".

Religious Statistics Rules and, in 1937, he and his followers refused to pay the hut tax. In August of that year, he wrote to Pegler:

> Look here, Government, I and my Christian followers, starting from today, shall never pay tax for the British kingdom.[35]

In order to avoid trouble from Gudu and his followers, the government gave Ana a Mulungu until the end of January 1938 to pay their taxes, when normally hut taxes should have been paid by the end of December 1937. During the month of January 1938, a Thyolo census clerk (Tom Sukali) went to Molere to assess the situation. The Ana a Mulungu told him:

> We are children of God and we cannot give you our names and our homes as we have done no wrong. Besides, why should we give you our names when you know that we have no food and are hungry because Government took away our gardens from us and gave them to other natives.[36]

By the end of January 1938 the Ana a Mulungu had not yet paid their hut taxes. Then, on 1 February 1938, a warrant was issued for the arrest of Gudu, who was charged with tax default. For two consecutive days, African police constables tried to arrest him, but failed because his followers crowded around, jostling the police. It was on the fourth day that the Thyolo District Inspector of Police, A.T. Tate, came in person and succeeded in arresting him. At first he wanted to walk to the Police station at the head of his hymn-singing adherents, but Tate persuaded him to ride in a Police vehicle instead.

At the trial, which was held on the following day, the authorities dropped the second charge of refusal to furnish the religious statistical information after he had pleaded ignorance. He was therefore found guilty of default of tax and sentenced to three months' imprisonment with hard labour. Thirty of his followers who came to the hearing and stated that they all wanted to go to prison as they too had not paid the hut tax, received sentences of three months' maximum imprisonment. During the trial some of them stood mute and refused to give their names.

---

[35] "Good to Pegler", August 1937, MNA, file no. IA/1413.
[36] Ibid.

Since Gudu and his followers refused to obey orders given by the district prison officers in Thyolo and Blantyre prisons, they were subsequently sent to the Central Prison in Zomba. There they continued to refuse to work or wear prison uniforms, but not for long, as they were put in solitary confinement for a period on bread and water. When, later, they revealed their names, it was found out that ten of the thirty had already paid their taxes and were eventually released. The others served their full sentences and, on discharge, returned to Thyolo District.[37]

While in prison, Gudu wrote a letter to W. Ormsby Gore, Secretary of State for the Colonies, complaining about the way he was being treated. When Ormsby Gore queried the case to the Governor, Harold Kittermaster, the reply he got could be understood as insisting that Gudu was a threat to the peace.[38] On 1 June 1938, Gudu was released from prison and returned to his *Zion ya Yehovah*.

Pegler warned Gudu that at the first sign of misbehaviour, he would be deported from his home district. But Gudu remained unrepentant and became even more defiant and overbearing than before. He not only embarked on a course of flouting the authority of Kaponda and Ntondeza, but also persuaded his followers to resist arrest by telling them that the action that had been taken in respect of the maize gardens relieved them of all obligations to pay tax.[39] In October 1938, he and his followers openly refused to pay tax. Warrants were issued for the arrest of Wilfrid Gudu and twenty-nine of his followers. On the morning of 4 November, an African police sergeant and six constables failed to arrest them, as they were truculent and insolent. That afternoon, Inspector Tate, Assistant Inspector Smith and twenty five men arrived on the scene. The following is Tate's account of what took place:

> When I arrived, I found Good and his followers in an open air enclosure; he was addressing them from a central stand. I told him to come quietly. His manner at once became insolent and truculent. He said that he would not go to the *boma* for me, for the District Commissioner or for anyone. He then went on about his gardens. I

---

37 Ibid.

38 Ibid. Letter from Governor Harold Kittermaster to Secretary of State for Colonies, W. Ormsby Gore, 13 May 1938.

39 MNA, file no. IA/1341; Boeder, "Wilfred Good and the Ana a Mulungu".

ordered the constables to take him. His followers closed in around us. Their manner was aggressive and insolent. They assaulted the police who tried to take him, many of whom were tripped up. Someone ripped my sleeve. Smith was bitten on the hand. It was becoming a riot ... and [they] were hurling remarks at us as follows: 'If you attempt to arrest me we will cut your throat and also the throat of that dog from Blantyre ... [referring to Smith].' At the same time Gudu drew his finger across his throat. 'You, and the rest of you are in this country to steal the wealth of natives. If you want war, you have it today ... [to the African policemen] you *askari*, why do you not join us and fight against the Europeans?'[40]

Seeing that Gudu was determined to resist arrest, Tate managed to arrest only some of his followers. Reinforcements were brought in by night from the neighbouring Mulanje District. That evening Major Pegler informed William B. Bithrey, Superintendent of Police for Southern Province, of Gudu's resistance to arrest. Bithrey came over from Blantyre to lead the assault force of eighty African constables and three other Europeans - Tate, Smith and Captain Branfill.

When the assault force arrived at *Zion ya Yehovah* on the following day, Gudu was standing in the doorway of his home carrying a Bible, and his followers in their white gowns stood around him in a pyramid structure with Gudu at the apex. Bithrey ordered Gudu to come along quietly, but he refused the order, called the police 'dogs', and said that he would obey only God's word. He went on to say that he would resist arrest with force, and advised the Europeans to return to their own country.

The police charged the crowd with drawn batons, and Gudu's followers responded with bites, blows, sticks and fists. Twenty-seven were arrested and taken before the Magistrate in Thyolo. Gudu and fifteen others were convicted and received maximum sentences of six months' hard labour for tax default, and three months' hard labour for assaulting the police, resisting arrest and obstructing court officers, to be served consecutively and not reduced. The remaining twelve were also convicted and served lesser sentences in Thyolo District gaol.[41]

---

[40] Inspector Tate to Superintendent of Police, 8 November 1938, MNA, file no. IA/1413.
[41] Ibid., testimony of William Barry Bithrey in matter of detention of Wilfrid Gudu.

A surviving member of the Ana a Mulungu church who underwent this ordeal with Gudu has given the following account:

On 5 November 1938 at about 4.00 am, a large group of policemen came in several trucks, carrying their guns, baton sticks, and short knives [*mabenesi*] and marched around the *Zion ya Yehovah*, while the leader yelled 'left, right'.

We were still at prayer in the *Kachisi* when the solders marched in and took Gudu and put him on their truck without hand-cuffing him. At the sound of a whistle, the policemen started beating us indiscriminately so hard that some bled, while others fainted. They handcuffed us, tied our legs, and threw us on their trucks like firewood. One policeman chanted triumphantly: 'Sokole! Sokole!' [Hip! Hip!] and the other policemen responded: 'Yoo!' [Hooray!]. The leader went on: 'Gudu zii!' [Defeat on Gudu!], and the response was: 'zii! [Defeat!]. The leader yelled 'Gavinala moto!' [Victory to the Governor!], and the response was 'Moto!' [Victory!]

As the trucks drove away, those who had fainted resuscitated. One of them chanted: 'Sokole! Sokole' [Hip! Hip!] and the others responded: 'Yoo! [Hooray!]. The cantor went on: 'Gavinala zii!' [Defeat on the Governor!] and the response was 'zii!' [Defeat]. Then the cantor yelled: 'Mulungu moto!' [Victory to God!] and the response was 'Moto!' [Victory!]. Then the chains which had been tied around Samson Chilembwe's neck broke and fell on the truck. Dodorowa's chain also broke and fell in like manner. When we arrived at Zomba Central Prison, the prison guard tried to open the prison doors so that we would enter, but the doors could not open. A senior prison warden took the keys from the guard but still the doors could not open. They called Gudu and asked him: 'Why do the doors not open?' Gudu replied: 'It is God Himself who has locked them.' We all slept outside that night. On the next morning, the prison guard told us to go and wash ourselves, but we said: 'We did not come here to wash ourselves.' At hearing this, the guard drove us forcefully to the place where there was water, and we washed ourselves.

A few high-ranking Europeans who had been driving to Zomba Prison to see the trouble-maker [Gudu] all died on the way in a car accident.[42]

---

[42] Samson Chilembwe. oral communication with the author at Zion Ana a Mulungu. Molere, 15 September 1984.

When the police searched Gudu's house, they found certain prohibited publications of the Watch Tower, such as: *Who shall rule the World?*, *The Kingdom and Vindication.*

The policemen remained on guard at the *Zion ya Yehovah*. Later, Gudu wrote a letter to the Secretary of State for the Colonies, Malcolm Macdonald, complaining that these policemen had raped his wife and the wives of his followers.[43]

The release of Gudu from Zomba Central Prison was to be effected on 21 June 1939, at the end of his sentence. But the new Governor, D.M. Kennedy, decided that he should be detained for less than five years under the provision of the Political Removal and Detention of Natives Ordinance, Chapter 25, of the Laws of Nyasaland. He was warned that if he ever left Zomba without permission, or failed to conduct himself to the Governor's satisfaction, he would be deported to a distant country.[44] The new Commissioner of Police, Bithrey, provided Gudu with a house at the Police Camp, some simple furniture, and two shillings per week to maintain himself. Gudu spent most of his time reading the Bible, marking passages which had close bearing to his plight.

According to a contemporary, Gudu was given a four-year gaol sentence. His duty was to go to the neighbouring villages to preach the word of God. He made many conversions. One day, he said to the prison warden:

> Set a blackboard in the open and ask all the high-ranking European government officials to come. Some writing from nowhere will appear on the blackboard. If the officials can read the writing, then let me be hanged. But it they fail to read it, know that your regime is doomed.

The warden told Gudu that the people he wished to see had refused to come, as they considered his motive ill-fated. Gudu responded:

> Although they have refused to turn up for this trial of strength, another person whose shoestrings I cannot untie, will come after me. When he comes, your regime will end because of your cruelty and injustice.[45]

---

[43] Testimony of William Barry Bithrey, MNA, file no. IA/1413.
[44] Ibid., minutes of Executive Council meeting of April 1939.
[45] Samson Chilembwe, oral communication with the author.

Gudu eventually become depressed as he pondered on the sufferings of his wife Maggie, and his seven children, while he himself went in rags. Bithrey wrote sympathetically to the Governor's Secretary: "I do not like the idea of the headquarters of the Police Force becoming a nudist colony."[46] Again in another letter he wrote: "Gudu should not be compelled to live in rags and to suffer the torment of realizing that his wife and family, from whom he is compulsorily separated, may be in want and penury."[47] Eventually, the administration decided to give one pound annually towards the purchase of Gudu's clothes. A suggestion that his wife and children join him did not come through for fear of loss of their gardens in Thyolo.

In early April 1941, Bithrey recommended that Gudu's case be reviewed after two years, and that he be released. But Pegler and Ntondeza felt that Gudu should not be allowed to return to Thyolo in the interests of peace. In May 1941, Governor Kennedy granted Gudu an interview during which he (Gudu) expressed all his troubles, particularly the issue of the maize garden. Gudu was allowed, in the following October, to spend ten days in Thyolo with his family. On 20 March 1942, Governor Kennedy - despite the opposition from Pegler, Eric Smith and Ntondeza - released Gudu, having admonished him to 'behave himself in every way'.[48]

When he returned to his *Zion ya Yehovah*, after initial reluctance he agreed to pay hut tax, but wanted to hand over a lump sum covering himself and thirteen of his followers. Smith disagreed with this arrangement, arguing that this type of procedure was not in keeping with the British system of individual rights. Gudu had no other alternative but to accept this explanation, although it had little relevance to him.

(vi)   Conscientious Objectors to Soil Conservation

After his release from detention, Gudu did not 'behave himself in every way' as Governor Kennedy had admonished him. Ten years later, he fell foul of the government regulations on soil conservation, apparently on religious grounds. After the Second World War, the colonial government took up the issue of soil conservation with determination and formulated

---

46 Commissioner of Police minutes of 20 February 1940, MNA, file no. IA/1413.

47 Ibid., Bithrey's letter of 15 March 1940.

48 Ibid., Kennedy, minutes of 30 March 1942.

policies which were to be implemented in all the districts by the Provincial Natural Resources Boards. Thus, in many districts, soil conservation bunding teams were concentrated into special areas and worked under close European supervision. Africans were employed, trained in the use of the Road Tracer and organized in teams of fourteen markers, with a European in charge of one or two such teams. The main work of the teams was the demarcation of contour bunds in selected areas, irrespective of garden boundaries, paths, compounds, grazing area, etc., and the construction of storm drains and check-dams where necessary. Staff of the Department of Agriculture pegged the contour line and hoed small marker ridges so that the line would not be lost through the removal of pegs. The garden owner was himself responsible for hoeing the bund within a specified time. It was the policy of all Boards to approach him in the first instance, pointing out the error of his ways and asking him to put the matter right before applying any direct administrative action.[49]

A tea planter in Thyolo, Arthur Westrop, has mentioned how difficult it was to convince the African population of the fact that soil conservation was necessary.[50] The Natural Resources Board's report of 1951 comments:

> It cannot be said that the African yet shows any sound appreciation of the necessity of soil conservation. It is generally a constant uphill battle requiring considerable administrative pressure to get the work done.
>
> It is to be hoped that, once the African knows that we mean business in this matter, he will be prepared to cooperate fully, whether he appreciates the importance of the work or not.[51]

Although resistance stemmed partly from popular conservatism, Gudu also advanced what may be termed 'conscientious' grounds, by which he meant religious objections for his refusal to cooperate with the Board authorities. The Bible, while enjoining man to cultivate the land, says nothing about bunding or ridging. A Bible text was quoted to the effect that "the waters of the earth shall run free".. Westrop goes on:

---

49 *Provincial Natural Resources Board: Annual Reports for the year 1951*, Zomba: Government Printer, 1952, p. 11.
50 Arthur Westrop, "Green Gold: a Story of a Tea Estate in Malawi", n.d.
51 *Provincial Natural Resources Board: Annual Report for the year 1951*, p. 11.

R.B. Royle, District Agricultural Officer
for Thyolo, 1952-1962

hence they opposed the contour ridges and bunds and insisted [sic]
on lining their crops up and down instead of across, the slope. The
consequent erosion and loss of soil can be imagined.[52]

As the *Zion ya Yehovah* was on a hill in a bend of the road, this meant that
during the wet season the road became covered in sheets of mud, preven-
ting lorries from passing by.

On the overall situation with regard to bunding in Thyolo District in
1952, the Board reported:

Three bunding teams operated in the District during the year and, as
a result of the fact that bunding was started in 1946 and the people

---

[52] Westrop, "Green Gold".

are aware of the benefits and with active support from the Administration, creditable progress has been made. Over three million yards of contours have been marked, covering some 11,500 acres and the majority of these have been made up to specification.[53]

The table below shows the extent of bunding operations in Thyolo and three adjacent districts:[54]

District	Length of bunds made up in yards		Area protected in acres	
	1951	1952	1951	1952
Thyolo	2,694,000	2,060,000	18,065	11,429
Mulanje	127,750	547,105	780	3,720
Blantyre	218,750	2,631,376	1,221	28,208
Zomba	40,250	105,600	214	5,000

However, on the darker side of this seemingly bright picture, the report has this to say:

> At the request of the Cholo District Natural Resources Board, an Order under Section 10 of the Ordinance was served on Wilfred Good, who occupies an area of African trust land in Cholo, but had refused to permit contours to be marked on his garden.[55]

Events which led to the escalation of the conflict between Gudu and the government officials were narrated to J.M. Schoffeleers by James David Moniwa, who worked as an agricultural instructor in Thyolo District between 1951 and 1966. The following account of the episode was kindly made available to me by Professor Schoffeleers.[56] The trouble started when William Jones was Agricultural Officer in Thyolo in 1950. R.B. Royle inherited it in 1952-1953 when it became very serious.

Moniwa was sent by Royle with a party of four overseers to Gudu. When the party met him he became very rude and said, in Chichewa: *"sindifuna kunena ndi ana"* (I don't want to talk to children). Neither did

---

[53] *Provincial Natural Resources Board: Annual Report for the year 1952*, p. 10.
[54] Source: *Provincial Natural Resources Boards: Annual Reports for the year 1951-1952.*
[55] *Ibid.*, 1952, p. 8.
[56] Oral communication, J.D. Moniwa to J.M. Schoffeleers, 23 September 1974.

he want to see Jones nor Royle. Royle telephoned the District Commissioner for Thyolo, D.M. Martin, who went to join the party. They found Gudu in his church with some of his followers, while others remained outside, answering his prayers. Those outside told him that the District Commissioner had arrived. Gudu came out without delay and greeted the District Commissioner, but not Royle and Jones whom he hated. Then Gudu had a private talk with Martin, who had his arm around Gudu's shoulders as a sign of friendship. Martin then told Royle and Jones to send their men up the next day to mark the bunds.

On the following day, the party came with some contract workers, but Gudu and his followers were not present. A sum of eleven pounds five shillings and seven pence (£11.5s.7.d) was spent on the work. Gudu, however, came later and started ridging through the bunds, once again breaking them. Moniwa reported the matter to Royle. No sooner had Royle heard the news that he came with Martin and a few policemen in a police car. Gudu refused to co-operate. They allowed him first to pray in his house with some of his followers, and thereafter he climbed into the police car with his books. Some of his followers wanted to go with him, but Martin refused.

After a week, Moniwa was called to the *boma* to give evidence in the case of Gudu at the magistrate's court. The Provincial Commissioner, W.H.J. Rangeley, and the new District Commissioner for Thyolo, Mr Sweetman, were present. Rangeley testified that he had signed an order to the effect that bunding should be made at Gudu's place. Gudu replied that this was only Rangeley's order, but that there had been no agreement. Royle reiterated what Rangeley had said. The magistrate ordered Gudu to make restitution of the money spent on the job. Gudu, however, defended himself most vigorously, basing his argument on the rights of private property. Moniwa explained the government regulation with regard to this case, but Gudu said he had nothing to do with it. He was then sentenced to three month's imprisonment for refusing to comply and pay the money. In his absence his followers, who continued to cultivate the land, completed the destruction of the bunds.

After his release from prison, Gudu is said to have been moved out of the *Zion ya Yehovah* to Bvumbwe, near Limbe, where he also got into trouble with the Central Africa Company, a tea-growing company. He was not allowed to cultivate any fields, and from then on depended on the common fund of his followers.

He eventually divorced his wife Maggie, and gradually married four other women, corresponding - as he put it - to the four corners of the world. This move disturbed some of his followers, and therefore many left him. He died on 14 March 1963, at the *Zion ya Yehovah*, and was succeeded as leader of the Ana a Mulungu by Gideoni Stivini.

(vii) Wilfrid Gudu and the Ana a Mulungu: A Critical Appraisal

Introduction

Wilfrid Gudu represents a totally new style of religious behaviour and religious protest in Malawi. I shall assess his unique ministry as preacher and leader of the Ana a Mulungu, concentrating on factors which drew people to him, and on his hostilities with the government administration. To put him in focus, I shall compare the origin of his *Zion ya Yehovah* with similar institutions in South Africa, and his style of leadership with that of John Chilembwe, who represents a different style.

For a deeper interpretation of Gudu's withdrawal from the society at large, I submit that it was a mechanism to stress the identity of his church both in terms of the world and of spiritual prospects. The suggestion that he was a nationalist agitator is a view advanced by the government administrators, arising mainly from the hostilities the background of which they did not fully understand.

The attraction of Gudu: preacher and visionary

Gudu's dissociation from the Malamulo Mission gave him a special symbolic status. He not only displayed for his supporters the inconsistencies in the Mission's practice but he also became the embodiment of their aspirations which were to be realized in the *Zion ya Yehovah*. He elevated himself to the level of a prophet or a visionary enforced by the mandate from God "to feed his flock at Molere", where the other Missions had failed. His symbols of power and authority were the two large wooden keys which he

THYOLO SOUTH

Thyolo Mountain Forest Reserve

THYOLO

BLANTYRE

Malamulo S.D.A. Mission

Kaponda

Makwasa

Khwethemule

Motheriwa

Molela R.C. Mission

ZIYONI YA YEHOVA

RUO

Masambanjati Forest Reserve

CHIKWAWA

Kalulu Hills Forest Reserve

Thekerani

SHIRE RIVER

ELEPHANT MARSH

BANGULA

BANGULA

BANGULA

0 1 2 3 4 5 Km

KEY

Mission	Other roads	
Trading centre	Railway	
Village	River	
Secondary road	Mountain/Hill	

Source: Department of Geography, Chancellor College, University of Malawi

wore around his neck, one for opening the gates of bondage here on earth, and the other for the portals of heaven. Indeed, he had become a 'Jesus Christ No. 2'. During religious services he often spoke with a guttural sound to stress that God spoke through him. This practice is similar to that found in some forms of spirit possession where the spirit speaks through its client in guttural sounds. Such messages carry much authority as they are considered to come from above. Gudu's prophetic vision is seen in the establishment of the *Zion ya Yehovah*. Thyolo District, in the throes of the emerging capitalist economy, created acute socio-economic problems for the ordinary people. With so much land alienated to the estate owners, many Africans became landless and were huddled on to the already over-crowded and less fertile crown land. Those who opted to stay on the estates were reduced to mere tenants and had to work in lieu of rent for the estate owners during certain periods of the year. The labour conditions on the estates were oppressive, not to mention the low wages the workers received. The large influx of Lomwe immigrants created fresh problems of adjustment to new conditions. Some sought employment in the estates while others tried to eke out an existence in the surrounding host villages.

According to Gudu, the missions which had been operating in the area had failed to stand up for the poor and the oppressed. Malamulo Mission had put the Ngoni late-comers in prominent positions in the Church and had followed their advice. The government administration had even elevated the chieftaincy of Ntondeza, the Makololo usurper.

The founding of *Zion ya Yehovah* was, then, to provide an alternative to the oppressive experience Gudu had undergone. He considered it a search for a Christianity of the soil, free from all the inconsistencies between doctrine and practice. By withdrawing from ordinary society, the new community would stress new relationships with the world and spiritual prospects without interference from outside, and thereby create its own identity. Intensely preoccupied with the assertion of a single sacred place, the Holy City of Jerusalem, the Old Testament evokes the joys of Zion in many psalms. The symbol of a 'Jerusalem' or 'Zion' which is a holy place, has encountered a lot of responses from the Africans who both re-enact and ritually celebrate it. Such New Jerusalems exist in many parts of Africa. They stretch from:

New Tawedzu in Ghana, the city of the Prophet Wovenu and the Apostolic Revelation Society, to Isaiah Shembe's Ekuphakameni in Natal; from N'kamba Jerusalem, Kimbangu's village in Zaire, to the Zion City of Bishop Mutendi by Mount Moria in Zimbabwe.[57]

In such communities there is one central headquarters with a wide range of activities to meet people's needs. One can go on pilgrimages, or even reside; be absorbed in lengthy and moving ceremonies of prayer; be healed of one's sickness and enjoy tranquillity of the soul.

The *Zion ya Yehovah* combined industrial zeal and religious piety within the broad framework of the Seventh-day Adventist tradition. Membership was drawn largely from the dispossessed and immigrants from Mozambique, mostly of the Lomwe sub-groups. Of the fifteen people who were sentenced to six months imprisonment for non-payment of tax and three months for obstructing court·officers, four were Mang'anja and eleven Lomwe from different villages under two chiefs, Ntondeza and Nsabwe.[58] Furthermore, the *Zion ya Yehovah* drew people from different villages. In 1940, the ten leading members came from five different villages under two chiefs, as the following diagram shows:[59]

Name of Chief (Traditional Authority)	Village	No. of leading members
1. Ntondeza	Mchacha	2
	Kaponda	5
2. Nsabwe	Nkhwangwa	1
	Katuli	1
	Mchenga	1

	Total	10

Members participated jointly in farming activities and various trades, thereby practicing the virtues of equity and justice which had been denied to many in the then obtaining socio-economic situation. Here the land was to be exploited by the whole community and its fruits enjoyed by all. Here, too, land became a stabilizing and unifying factor in contrast to the land issue which had created a great deal of unrest in the area, especially

---

57 Adrian Hastings, *African Christianity*, London: Geoffrey Chapman, 1976, p. 26.
58 MNA, file no. IA/1341; Boeder, "Wilfred Good and the Ana a Mulungu".
59 MNA, file no. IA/1341.

through the ignominious practice of *thangata*. There was also the issue of low wages in the estates. Gudu once complained:

> When we work for the Europeans they give us little money, but they themselves get £90 or £100 every year.[60]

In his community there were no wages, undue competition or petty jealousies as members pooled their resources.

However, the main centre of attraction was Gudu himself. One of his early followers said:

> I believe that Wilfrid Gudu talks to God, and God talks to him, and because of this I would do anything that he told me.[61]

Not surprisingly, therefore, some of his followers claimed God had told them in dreams to join Gudu, and so there was no need to consult their traditional rulers; only Gudu mattered, as he was divinely appointed leader of the new community. Gudu's leadership is symbolically represented by the position of his house being on top of the hill, and those of his followers below, and also by the position of his pulpit at the top end of his church. He wore a special dress which distinguished him from his followers. In his heyday of popularity, Kaponda admitted that, "even since he has been imprisoned, more are coming. I do not understand why, unless it is because they think they will evade tax."[62] Feeling threatened at the prospect of Gudu's return, he said: "If he comes back to my village, I must move somewhere else."[63]

According to Gudu, the Europeans manipulated the Word of God to oppress the people, and hence they did not practise what they taught. In his search for a liberating gospel, he felt he had to dissociate himself in word and symbol from what he considered a manifest distortion of the Word of God. He raised the school-fee question in a manner reminiscent of Kamwana's objection against the Livingstonia Mission in 1909. However strange this allegation might sound, we have to understand that, until recently, school and church were considered synonymous. Mission schools generally required their pupils to be members of the mission's denomination.

---

60 Report on Native Controlled Missions, MNA, file no, IA/1339.
61 Statement by Gidioni Stivini, 1938. MNA. file no. IA/1413.
62 Ibid.
63 Ibid.

Mission school teachers were also considered as part-time catechists or evangelists of their respective missions. In-so-far as schools were recruiting agencies and evangelistic institutions for the various denominations so, according to Gudu, no fees should be demanded.

Regarding himself as having a mandate to preach the gospel polluted by the white men, Gudu despised what appeared to him a projection of European influence. He proudly declared: "I wear the cloth made in England when I go to hoe my garden."[64] And again: "If I am removed from my area, I should not be sent to where other Europeans are."[65] Despite these outbursts against Europeans, Gudu accepted the Christian message which they brought.

Cooperation in his *Zion ya Yehovah* was remarkable. Members were strengthened by a life of prayer which also provided them with a certain sense of security and even immunity from evil forces, such as witchcraft and sorcery. The name Ana a Mulungu emphasized the idea of being a select group destined for salvation starting here and now. Membership of the group conferred a special status and identity symbolized by the special uniforms worn during church services. Having a house built near to that of Gudu provided legitimation of the incumbent's social position in that he was near "a man who could talk to God".

Gudu had, in the traditional context, established a real *Mbumba*, an extended family unit, which was the focus of all relationships. In the *Mbumba*, all members are related to one another either by kinship, putative or real, or by affinity. Outsiders can be coopted into any relationship which is suitable to them. As production and consumption rely on reciprocity, each member feels responsible for the welfare of the other, and vice versa. The community's property is at the disposal of all incumbents, who use it for the good of the community. Conflicts are settled amicably by the *mwini mbumba* (head of the family) or *nkhoswe* (guardian) who calls for a *bwalo* (court session at which opposing parties lay their claims and the matter is settled by general consensus).[66]

---

64 Report on Native Controlled Missions, MNA, file no. IA/1339.
65 Inspector Tate to Superintendent of Police, 8 November 1938, MNA, file no. IA/1413.
66 Tew, *People of the Lake Nyasa Region*, p. 43.

Gudu was addressed as *bambo* (father) and other members call one another brother, sister, mother, etc., to stress their belonging to one community, the *Zion ya Yehovah*.[67]

The maize garden issue: an assessment

The hut tax issue which was triggered by the conflict on the maize garden, has been interpreted by Rotberg, Boeder and others as the religious expression of the rise of nationalism within a rural context. None among these writers mention the conflict around the soil conservation policies in 1952/53. Commenting on the prospects of Gudu's career after his release from detention, Rotberg writes: "his day, in fact, had passed."[68]

Gudu did not claim to be a nationalist and there is no evidence to suggest that his followers considered him to be such. His refusal to pay the hut tax was not on nationalistic grounds but was directly linked with the maize garden issue which, in turn, reinforced his withdrawal into his total community. He felt that the judgment on his case given by the magistrate's court at Thyolo was a betrayal of Christian principles of justice by the white people (or government) who professed to abide by them. What pained him most was that the magistrate had been corrupted by Ntondeza and Kaponda, who prevented a proper hearing of the case. Gudu was convinced that his claim of ownership of the garden was legitimate, and that the court had not been justified in taking it away from him and giving it to the other party. According to local custom, even if it were proven beyond reasonable doubt that the garden did not actually belong to Gudu, the decision to return the garden should have been deferred until after harvest time. But the court ordered the immediate return of the garden to the other party before the maize crop had been harvested. Both Kaponda and Ntondeza knew the customary procedure but did not intervene. It is most probable that the magistrate simply acted in the interests of maintaining law and order. But it was not long before he realized that Gudu did not see it in the same way. Gudu retaliated by refusing to pay the hut tax, claiming that he had been deprived of the means to do so. His disappointment with the

---

[67] Oral communication, Willie Kasonga, Mafunga Village, T.A. Changata, 15 September 1984.
[68] Rotberg, *The Rise of Nationalism in Central Africa*, p. 154.

administration of justice led him to flout openly the authority of Kaponda and Ntondeza.

The content of his dream in which God told him that tax payers are 'Sons of Evil, non-taxpayers the Sons of God' reinforced his religious motive for not collaborating with the government. For him, taxpaying in-so-far as it symbolized collaboration with the perpetrators of injustice and oppression - Europeans and their allies, such as Kaponda and Ntondeza - would be putting oneself in the category of 'Sons of Evil'. The dream could have been a legitimating rationalization of the position that he had adopted. Turning to the colonial administrators, Gudu said angrily:

> I thought you were the servants of God as the Bible says, that is why
> I was paying taxes, but now I realize you are not servants of God.[69]

The authorities interpreted Gudu's activities as political because, in a densely populated area, they feared a large-scale revolt, were his influence to spread. The Governor, Harold Kittermaster, commented:

> His refusal to obey the orders of Government as well as his wild and
> subversive statements that he recognized no Government, but only
> the will of God, have created a certain amount of political excitement
> in Thyolo District and possibly in neighbouring areas as well.[70]

On the origin of Gudu's intransigence, the Commissioner of Police noted:

> There is little doubt that his attitude towards Government and recog-
> nized authority was influenced by this literature [alluding to the
> Watch Tower publications found in Gudu's house after his arrest]
> which, as is well known, extols the passive resistance to all govern-
> ments.[71]

There is no doubt that Gudu read some Watch Tower literature which was in wide circulation at that time. He must have followed what had been going on in the Watch Tower Movement. But there is no clear evidence to suggest that his refusal to pay the hut tax had been directly influenced by the Watch Tower literature. Had that been so, one could not explain his claims that he had intended to pay the hut tax from the sale of the maize

---

[69] Good to Government, Cholo, 2 February 1938, MNA, file no. IA/1413.

[70] Ibid., Letter from Governor Harold Kittermaster.

[71] MNA, file no. IA/1341.

harvest, and the fact that he eventually did start paying. The Police Commissioner's assertions have to be seen in the colonial administrator's perspective which branded any open defiance or opposition to the government as Watch Tower - inspired, since this religious group had had several conflicts with the government during the inter-war period.

The soil conservation issue: an assessment

In the conflict over the soil conservation exercises, Gudu clearly came out with the Bible to support his stance. Was it merely biblical fundamentalism or distrust of the new ways which made Gudu refuse to submit to the agricultural policies? It is known that the Watch Tower Movement on several occasions used the same biblical arguments to refuse to submit to the new ways of soil conservation which were being enforced country-wide, sometimes ruthlessly.[72]

The ordinary people who, for a long time, had been accustomed to shifting cultivation, deeply resented these new methods of agriculture popularly known as *malimidwe* especially for the harsh way in which they were being implemented. Perhaps Gudu's negative attitude towards the reforms was motivated by his religious conviction that the old ways of farming which symbolized traditional values uncontaminated by European influence were God-given, since they could find biblical support. It was in the late 1950s that the nationalist movement in Malawi took up the implementation of the soil conservation policies as a real political issue.

Wilfrid Gudu in focus

The situation in Thyolo during Gudu's time began to look like that of apartheid South Africa. Sundkler writes:

> One should not forget the other dimension of the alienation crisis among the African masses [in South Africa]: the experience of being deprived of their land, suddenly finding themselves landless and forced to serve as squatters on Boer farms ... The Natives Land Act of 1913 had a traumatic effect ... It was in this situation, in the city, on the farms, and in the reserves, that search for a new identity went

---

[72] Oral communication. Ronald Sukwambe, Namulenga, Mulanje, 3 December 1983.

on ... The luminary visions in Zulu dream life formed a new and obvious point of reference: the Zionist group in white.[73]

Hence the policy of separate development in South Africa is to a great extent responsible for the formation of total religious communities or 'Zions' on land either bought or leased. Daniel Nkoyane's Zion, Zion City of Lekganyane, and Isaiah Shembe's Ekuphakameni are among the well-known communities.

Gudu wanted to counteract what was developing as a kind of apartheid by placing himself outside the society at large. Like the South African prophets, he founded the *Zion ya Yehovah* as a separate village and resisted interference or encroachment from outside; hence the bitter fight about the maize garden and the soil conservation issues. Although Gudu and Chilembwe led their respective churches at different periods (Chilembwe: 1900-1915, and Gudu: 1938-63), their styles of religious independency have certain resemblances as well as discrepancies. I shall point out a few areas in order to draw a comparison between them. The justification of this comparison is to emphasize that each leader had his unique style of inculcating the ideas of religious independency among his followers. One of the first spheres in which Africans could gain independence of white control was through separatist churches.

Shepperson and Price have traced Chilembwe's formative period to his tutelage under Joseph Booth and his education in America where he became a Baptist minister in an American Negro Church.[74] From Booth, Chilembwe undoubtedly heard about the ideal of 'Africa for the Africans' and the ideas about a just land settlement in Africa.[75] In America, Chilembwe attained a high standard of education which made him conversant with the burning issues of the time, such as racial segregation, the uplifting of the black man, and the evils of colonialism.[76] His continued links with the American Negro Baptists reinforced his critical feelings towards white men. He opened his mission in Malawi in 1900 as a missionary among his own people.

---

[73] B. Sundkler, *Zulu Zion and some Swazi Zionist*, London: Oxford University Press, 1976, p. 311.
[74] Shepperson and Price, *Independent African*.
[75] Booth published his views in America while Chilembwe was there; Joseph Booth, *Africa for the African*, 1897, reprint edited by Laura Perry, Blantyre: CLAIM, 1996.
[76] Langworthy, *"Africa for the African"*, pp. 93-109.

Gudu on the other hand was a teacher with elementary education from the Malamulo Mission, which had a tendency to segregate its African staff and keep it under total subjection. Furthermore, the Malamulo Mission had inward-looking policies with little sympathy for the oppressed lot within its precincts. The circumstances of Gudu's secession from the Malamulo Mission are regarded by his followers as a revelation. Gudu himself is considered to be a prophet and a visionary who was to inaugurate a new era and a breakthrough in evangelization.

As religious leaders in their own time and place, both Chilembwe and Gudu were faced with a deteriorating socio-economic situation. Drought, famine and the growth of millennial expectations were added to the growing international unrest.

Most of Chilembwe's followers worked or lived on the vast A.L. Bruce estates. There was the tenant system which stipulated that people work in lieu of paying rent. The labour roll books of the estates show that the safeguards laid down in the "Employment of Natives Ordinance" for ensuring the proper payment of African labourers were not complied with. The policy of the management of the estates did not allow any Christian churches on the land, and therefore applications by Chilembwe for leave to build churches and schools were refused. One or two churches which were built by his followers without permission were destroyed by William P. Livingstone, the manager. When the people complained to Mr Cruise, the Assistant Magistrate at Chiradzulu, he supported Livingstone's action.

The proximity of Chilembwe's headquarters to Bruce estates, his unfriendly relations with the management of the estates, and the unsatisfactory conditions prevailing on the estates, were a constant source of discontent and conflict. However, Chilembwe's orientation was, even in 1911, "the Booker T. Washington 'petit-bourgeois' ideal, not that of the militant revolutionary".[77] He had several schools, had attempted cooperative schemes, and had provided sewing classes for women. He aimed at creating an independent industrial organization for Africans. Inevitably, such ideals were neither acceptable to, nor understood by, the European planters. He created an open community with its tentacles spread to win the confidence of leaders of other independent churches. He was on good terms

---

[77] Shepperson and Price, *Independent African*, pp. 146, 170.

with the Church of Scotland Mission at Blantyre and kept in touch with some of its leading African ministers. Therefore he had undoubtedly exceptional administrative gifts, and by these means he succeeded in acquiring an ascendancy over a number of churches in his area.[78] But he was neither a prophet nor did he claim to have any special charisma as a messiah. His followers regarded him as a pastor and leader who had profound knowledge about the local situation and the world at large.

Gudu lived in much the same situation in Thyolo District where land alienation, exploitation of labour and the *thangata* system were rampant, as the country was desperately trying to recover from the Great Depression. When he founded the Ana a Mulungu, he quickly withdrew from the society at large to a closed community. There he devised a particular mode of living with its own special symbols, e.g. wearing of hand-made white garments, rearing white chickens only, etc. His followers were not allowed to be in contact with the outside world, as Chilembwe's followers were. Gudu assumed the role of a prophet and a father-figure who was believed to be in contact with God. Many stories about his *mirabilia* are still recounted today by his followers. Like Chilembwe, he espoused the creation of an independent industrial organization, but this was restricted to his followers. Gudu did not want to have anything to do with either the Malamulo Mission or the colonial government, let alone the local chiefs, as he had opted for a closed community.

Chilembwe's initial response to the morbid situation was to publicly condemn and denounce the prevailing injustices. The colonial government took no notice of his criticisms and introduced no reforms. Then, in 1915, he resorted to violence. His motives for the uprising have been a subject of debate among writers, but today he is popularly and widely hailed as a proto-nationalist and a political martyr.

Gudu on the other hand denounced government action when provoked. His followers resorted to violence against the police to protest against Gudu's arrest. They have interpreted his trial and sufferings in jail as a triumph over injustice, and have shown how the power of God was manifested throughout these episodes. But the white administrators' view of Gudu was that he was an egotist and had an anti-government attitude. Gov-

---

[78] D.D. Phiri, *John Chilembwe*, Limbe: Longman, 1975, pp. 32, 34.

ernor Harold Kittermaster described him as "an individual of fanatical temperament and antagonistic mentality".

In summary, we may note that Chilembwe and Gudu had different backgrounds of formation for their roles. Chilembwe had already been in touch with the wider world during his stay in America. He geared his community towards a meaningful survival in a confused but changing society. Gudu, however, came from a mission which had espoused a ghetto mentality and only addressed itself to issues of short-range benefit to the African. As leader of the Ana a Mulungu, he considered it best to drift away from the society at large and form a close-knit community where he would be free from interference and realize his Christian ideals.

Both Chilembwe and Gudu had in common the fact that the appeal of their churches lay in what was congenial to their flock which was drawn from a cross-section of ethnic groups. However, as their styles differed, Chilembwe elicited a conversionist response which implied that his followers had to change their attitudes in order to be saved from evil and corruption. Therefore, he attracted the emerging elite, people who had attained a reasonably high education, or those who espoused change positively by earnestly trying to improve their own lot through the opportunities that were available. Gudu, on the other hand, elicited an introversionist response, whereby salvation is seen in terms of withdrawal from the evil world. His followers came mainly from the ordinary folk, people with little or no school at all, whose response to change was rather negative in-so-far as they had not much to gain, or thought there was not much to gain, in both the emerging capitalist economy and the traditional set-up.

Finally, Wishlade says that no sects in this part of the country (Malawi) are today led by prophets or messiahs.[79] Gudu's career seems to me a case in point far refuting his statement. Arguably, Gudu has very much the makings of a prophet. Perhaps Wishlade did not get any facts about the Ana a Mulungu. The 'Sons of God' he mentions were a different church organization and should therefore not be confused with Gudu's movement.

---

[79] R.L. Wishlade, *Sectarianism in Southern Nyasaland*, London: Oxford University Press for the International African Institute, 1965, p. 42.

Conclusion

In conclusion, the career of Wilfrid Gudu as founder of the Ana a Mulungu church shows that he was a courageous leader, but perhaps somewhat fanatical in the eyes of those who did not follow him. As a preacher and a visionary unparalleled in the history of religious independency in Malawi, he formed the *Zion ya Yehovah*, a total religious institution, in an attempt to re-define Christian identity in terms of the situation in Thyolo District. In the grip of a rapidly expanding capitalist economy, vital to the post-depression economic revival of the country, Thyolo District experienced severe socio-economic problems such as land alienation, the tenant system, overcrowding, internal migratory labour, low wages and other causes of unrest. Gudu considered himself as having a mandate from God to liberate his people from the injustices and hypocrisy of the missions, the colonial administrators and their collaborators. Although his message was not very clear, he expressed himself in words and symbols which earned him high esteem from his followers, although at times they sounded subversive to the administrators. The maize garden issue which sparked off the initial conflict, shows "how personalities could affect the quality of justice in colonial Malawi".[80]

In retrospect, the confrontations show how far the colonial administrators failed to grasp the real motive of the introversionist and visionary. They merely translated it into political terms. A note by the Commissioner of Police at that time suggests that the government administration had not fully grasped the motive behind Gudu's behaviour:

> I find him an interesting personality, intelligent above the average, and with great sincerity of purpose. I feel sure that there have been misunderstandings in the past, and that the attitude of his followers in his clash with Government was engendered by a sense of loyalty to their 'head'.[81]

Even Governor Kennedy admitted that the Gudu affair had not been handled fairly. He wrote:

---

[80] Boeder, "Wilfred Good and the Ana a Mulungu", p. 17.
[81] MNA, file no. IA/1341.

All through this business I have been a little unhappy as to the manner in which Good was handled in the first instance. With the utmost appreciation of his many good qualities, I must express the opinion that Mr Pegler has very little political instinct: what he has is derived from the technique which obtains to the south of us.[82]

I have suggested that, as Gudu and his Ana a Mulungu withdrew into a total community, by which their identity was reinforced, in consequence the attitude of the group on the one hand, and those of traditional rulers and the colonial authorities on the other, became polarized. The *Zion ya Yehovah* is, in a way, a structural representation of religious protest to the prevailing conditions.

Makwasa in southern Thyolo is today a leading banana growing area. Banana plantations are a viable means of soil conservation.

---

[82] Ibid., Kennedy, memorandum of 30 March 1942. Boeder, ("Wilfred Good and the Ana a Mulungu"), heard from G.D. Hayes on 22 June 1981 that Pelger was born in South Africa, was a cricket player for the national side, and served with the South African forces in France during World War I.

Select Bibliography

Boeder, R.B., "Wilfred Good and the Ana a Mulungu", History seminar paper, no.3, Chancellor College, University of Malawi, 1981-1982.

Chakanza, J.C., "An Annotated List of Independent Churches in Malawi, 1900-1981", *Sources for the Study of Religion in Malawi*, no. 10 (December 1983).

Chidzero, C.Z., "Thangata in Northern Thyolo District: A Socio-economic Study in Chimaliro and Bvumbwe Area", History seminar paper, no. 13, Chancellor College, University of Malawi, 1980-1981.

Chirwa, W.C., "Masokwa Elliot Kenan Kamwana Chirwa: His Religious and Political Activities, and the Effects of Kamwanaism in South-east Nkhata Bay, 1908-1956", unpublished, History seminar paper, Chancellor College, University of Malawi, 1984.

Chirwa, W.C., "Masokwa Elliot Kenan Kamwana Chirwa: His Religious and Political Activities, and Impact in Nkhata Bay, 1908-1956", *Journal of Social Science*, (Zomba), Vol. 12 (1985), pp. 21-43.

Cole, M., *Jehovah's Witnesses: The New World Society*, New York: Vantage Press, 1955.

Cross, S., "Independent Churches and Independent States: the Jehovah's Witnesses in East and Central Africa", unpublished paper.

Cross, S., "Social History and Millennial Movements: The Watch Tower in South Central Africa", *Social Compass*, Vol. XXIV (1977), pp. 83-95.

Cross, S., "The Watch Tower Movement in South Central Africa 1908-45", unpublished D. Phil., Oxon., 1973.

Cross, S., "The Watch Tower, Witch-cleansing and Secret Societies in Central Africa", paper read at Lusaka Conference on the History of Central African Religions, 1974.

Elmslie, W.A., "Ethiopianism in Nyasaland", *Livingstonia News*, Vol. 2/5 (October 1909).

Goffman, E., *Asylums: Essays on the Social Situation of Mental Patients and Other Inmates*, New York: Anchor Books, 1961.

Greschat, H-J., "Kitawala, the Origins, Expansion and Religious Beliefs of the Watch Tower Movement in Central Africa", unpublished, Ph.D., Marburg, 1967.

Hastings, A., *A History of African Christianity, 1950-57*, London: Cambridge University Press, 1979.

Hastings, A., *African Christianity*, London: Geoffrey Chapman, 1976.

Hooker, J.R., "Witnesses and Watch Tower in the Rhodesias and Nyasaland", *Journal of African History*, Vol. VI/I (1965), pp. 91-106.

Kambuwa, A., "Malawi: Ancient and Modern History," unpublished manuscript, Zomba: University of Malawi Library, n.d.

Khanje, C.K., "Impact of Malamulo Mission in Southern Thyolo 1902-1972: A Broad Perspective", History seminar paper, no. 3, Chancellor College, University of Malawi, 1972-1973.

Langworthy, H., *"Africa for the African": The Life of Joseph Booth*, Blantyre: CLAIM, 1996.

Linden, I. and J., "Chiefs and Pastors in the Ntcheu Rising of 1915", in R.J. MacDonald, *From Nyasaland to Malawi: Studies in Colonial History*, Nairobi: East African Publishing House, 1975.

MacDonald, R.J., "A History of African Education in Nyasaland 1875-1945", Ph.D., Edinburgh, 1969.

McCracken, J.K., "The Livingstonia Mission and the Origins of the Watch Tower Movement in Central Africa", unpublished paper, October 1964.

McCracken, J.K., *Politics and Christianity in Malawi 1875-1940*, London: Cambridge University Press, 1977.

McMinn, R.D., "The First Wave of Ethiopianism", *Livingstonia News*, Vol. 2/4 (October 1909).

Onselen, C. van, *Chibaro: African Mine Labour in Southern Rhodesia 1900-1933*, London: Pluto Press, 1976.

Pachai, B., *Land and Politics in Malawi, 1875-1975*, Kingston, Ontario: Limestone Press, 1978.

Pachai, B., "The State and the Churches in Malawi during Early Protectorate Rule", *Journal of Social Science*, (Malawi), Vol. 1 (1972), pp. 7-27.

Phiri, B.M.N., "Independent Churches in Nkhata Bay District", History seminar paper, Chancellor College, University of Malawi, 1970.

Phiri, D.D., *John Chilembwe*, Limbe: Longman, 1975.

Proceedings of the Nyasaland United Missionary Conference 1900.

Ranger, T.O., *The African Churches of Tanzania*, Historical Association of Tanzania, paper no. 5, Nairobi: East African Publishing House, n.d.

Ranger, T.O., "The Early History of Independency in Southern Rhodesia", *Religion in Africa*, proceedings of a seminar held in the Centre of African Studies, University of Edinburgh, 10-12 April 1964.

Ranger, T.O., "The Mwana Lesa Movement of 1925", in T.O. Ranger and John Weller (eds.), *Themes in the Christian History of Central Africa*, London: Heinemann, 1975, pp. 45-75.

Robinson, V.E., *History of the South-East African Union*, unpublished typescript, South East Africa Union of Seventh-day Adventists, Blantyre, 1952.

Rotberg, R.I., *The Rise of Nationalism in Central Africa: The Making of Malawi and Zambia: 1873-1964*, Cambridge, Mass.: Harvard University Press, 1967.

Russell, C.T., *Studies in Scriptures: IV, The Battle of Armageddon*, Brooklyn, 1897.

Shepperson, G. and Price, T., *Independent African: John Chilembwe and the Origins, Setting and Significance of the Nyasaland Native Rising of 1915*, Edinburgh: Edinburgh University Press, 1958.

Shepperson, G.A., "Nyasaland and the Millennium", in S.L. Thrupp (ed.), *Millennial Dreams in Action - Essays in Comparative Study*, The Hague: Mouton, 1962.

Sundkler, B., *Zulu Zion and some Swazi Zionist*, London: Oxford University Press, 1976.

Tew, M., *Peoples of the Lake Nyasa Region*, London: Oxford University Press, 1950.

Turner, H.W., *Religious Innovation in Africa: Collected Essays on New Religious Movements*, Boston: G.K. Hall and Co., 1979.

Westrop, A., "Green Gold: a Story of a Tea Estate in Malawi", n.d.

Wishlade, R.L., *Sectarianism in Southern Nyasaland*, London: Oxford University Press for the International African Institute, 1965.

Index

101

King's African Rifles 50
Kittermaster, Harold 73, 89, 94
Kololo 84
Kore-Kore Reserve 33
Kusita, Wilson Daniel 29
Lala 31, 48
Lamba 31, 48
Land alienation 10, 54, 93, 95
Langworthy, Harry 13
Laws of Nyasaland 76
Leiden 11
Lettow-Vorbeck, von 35
Limbe 29, 63, 81
Linden, Ian and Jane 55
Linjisi 29
Lisale 39F
Livingstone, William P. 92
Livingstonia News 17, 52
Livingstonia 15, 23, 48; Mission 10, 13, 16f, 19, 21f, 43ff, 47, 49, 51, 52f, 86
Liwonde 28
Logamundi District 33, 47
Lomwe 10, 60, 85; immigration 60, 84; sub-groups 59, 85
Louden Mission (Embangweni) 44
Lower Shire Valley 13, 28
Luapula 31, 38
Lunar months 68
Lunda 38
Macalpine, Rev. A. 15, 18, 23, 43
Macdonald, Malcolm 76
MacDonald, R.J. 12
Machinga 58
Machiringa Village 63
Maize 61, 70; garden 69, 73, 77, 88, 91
Maize garden issue 69-77, 88, 95
Makololo 84
Malabvi 63
Malamulo Mission (SDA) 10, 15, 59, 63ff, 63n, 69, 82, 84, 92f
Malimidwe 90
Mambwe 31, 35
Manda, Anna 26
Manda, J.D. 13

Manda, James Stanley 32n
Mandala 15
Mang'anja 59f, 63f, 85
Mankhambira, Chief 26, 54
Manono Tin Mine 37
Marengamzoma, Chief 54
Martin, D.M. 81
Maseko Ngoni 55
Mashona Gold Field 38
Mashona 33
Masonga, Phillip 63
Matandani Mission (SDA) 63
Mauritius 26
Mazoe 32
Mbozi District 35
Mbumba 87
McCracken, John 12, 18, 43f, 53f
Mchacha Village 85
Mchape 12, 12n
Mchenga Village 85
Mchimi 39, 51f
McLukie, R.A. 26, 30, 30n
Medical charms 34; charms 21, **34f**
Medicine, protective 35; traditional 41; western 41
Members of Parliament 18
Migrant workers 27, 47
Migratory labour 95
Millenial doctrine 48; expectations 49, 52, 92; Kingdom 21; language 38
Millennarian views 19
millennialism 45
Millennium 28, 45f
Mines 16, 31, 38, 52
Mining areas 13, 32
Ministry 9ff, 13f, 16, 38f, 41, 43, 53, 82
Mirabilia 93
Misasa 40, 40n
Mission discipline 47
Missionary conferences 17
Mkandawire, Yaphet Mponda 54
Mnkhwakwata, Robert 39, 43
Moggeridge, L.T. 53
Molere 11, 64f, 72, 82
Moniwa, James David 80f

103

105

Printed in the United States
By Bookmasters